S0-AGL-749

WILDFLOWER
GARDENS

60 Spectacular Plants and How To Grow Them in Your Garden

C. Colston Burrell-Guest Editor

Cover photograph: Coreopsis and Culver's root
Left: Harlequin lupine and miniature lupine

FOR THE
ADVANCE
MENT OF
BOTANY
AND THE
SERVICE OF
THE CITY

BROOKLYN
BOTANIC
GARDEN
PUBLICATIONS
· MCMXCVIII ·

Janet Marinelli
SERIES EDITOR

Jane Ludlam
MANAGING EDITOR

Bekka Lindstrom
ART DIRECTOR

Judith D. Zuk
PRESIDENT

Elizabeth Scholtz
DIRECTOR EMERITUS

Handbook #159
Copyright © Summer 1999 by the Brooklyn Botanic Garden, Inc.
Handbooks in the *21st-Century Gardening Series,* formerly *Plants & Gardens,*
are published quarterly at 1000 Washington Ave., Brooklyn, NY 11225.
Subscription included in Brooklyn Botanic Garden subscriber membership dues ($35.00 per year).
ISSN # 0362-5850   ISBN # 1-889538-11-6
Printed by Science Press, a division of the Mack Printing Group

TABLE OF CONTENTS

WILDFLOWER GARDENS:

Nature and Nurture

by C. Colston Burrell

NATIVE WILDFLOWERS ARE AMONG the loveliest parts of the natural landscape. They grace fields, woodlands, wetlands, beaches, and rocky mountain slopes. Sweeps of bluebells and trout lilies carpet the ground on a woodland floor. Joe-pye weed and swamp sunflower enliven a moist roadside. In the spring, even the deserts of the Southwest come alive with wildflowers, while in the fall, eastern meadows are awash with goldenrods and asters.

Many wildflowers are also well suited to the cultivated landscape, and there are lots of good reasons to use wildflowers in gardens. Gardeners love color, and we love to bring the beauty of nature into our yards. Growing wildflowers enables us to do both. Another important reason to use native plants is to preserve the character of our regions. The best way to keep the visual sense of place that makes Minneapolis different from Atlanta or Washington, D.C., is to use the local flora. As Wilhelm Miller wrote in his 1915 treatise *The Prairie Spirit in Landscape Gardening,* "The Illinois rose beside the door is beautiful in itself and every year it will come to mean more to every passerby because it will suggest pleasant thoughts of Illinois." The same could be said about other plants and other regions of the country. What's more, native wildflowers foster and support

The beauty of many wildflower-strewn natural landscapes, like this lupine field on the rocky slopes near Mount Rainier, is easy to bring home to the garden.

the maximum diversity of associated plants and animals.

To use wildflowers effectively in the garden, it's not necessary to recreate down to the smallest detail habitats found in nature. This book shows how to incorporate wildflowers in meadows as well as beds and borders and other traditional garden designs. Whether its style is naturalistic or quite formal, however, a wildflower garden should grow out of the site's ecology. "A Gardener's Ecology" covers the ecological processes that should inform the wildflower garden—or any garden. Nature's patterns are also a rich source of inspiration for garden design, and "Designing With Nature" explains how to capture the visual essence of a natural scene by understanding the spatial patterns, both vertical and horizontal, that exist in natural plant communities.

The gardens profiled in the "Portfolio" section are living proof that wildflower gardens can have many styles, from formal to wild. Finally, "The Best American Plants for Wildflower Gardens" profiles the stars of these beautiful landscapes—60 spectacular plants that are adapted to the widest range of garden conditions. For easy reference, the plants are grouped according to their light requirements: shade, partial shade, and sun.

The wildflower garden is evidence of a new garden aesthetic based on regional landscapes and plants, a blend of nature and nurture, and a partnership between a gardener and the forces of nature. Each home landscape is part of the system and each gardener has a part to play. Ecology can be beautiful.

A GARDENER'S ECOLOGY

by Henry W. Art

THE GROWING INTEREST in wildflower gardens is part of the age-old quest for the "right plant for the right spot." Native plant gardens that are designed to take advantage of local conditions and reflect prevailing ecological processes often are less hassle than high-maintenance, formal beds and borders, and they blend more gracefully into the landscape.

The key to successful wildflower gardening is to keep in mind a few basic ecological considerations, such as variations in local climatic conditions, the structures of plant communities, and soil characteristics. Change is also a natural process that influences wildflower gardens. You should expect that over the long haul weeds will invade, plants will grow, plants will die, and desirable native "volunteers" will find your garden a welcome habitat.

LET NATURE BE YOUR GUIDE

Naturally occurring plant "communities" provide the clues to the kinds of wildflower gardens that might be successful where you live. The natural vegetation varies enormously from region to region, reflecting differ-

Virginia bluebells are adapted to the sunlight that strikes the floor of this deciduous forest in spring before the canopy leafs out. Look to nearby forests or fields for clues to successful local wildflower gardening.

ences in the climate and soils. While a meadow garden of annual wildflowers and grasses may successfully endure for many decades in southern California, it is unlikely to persist for much more than a single growing season in the East. Likewise, it would be nearly impossible to grow a garden of eastern woodland spring perennials in the Southwest deserts. Different species are adapted to different sets of environmental conditions, so choose the plants that are going to be most at home in your garden.

Regional patterns of temperature and precipitation play a major role in determining the kinds of vegetation that grow. Forests are generally found in regions with abundant precipitation distributed relatively evenly throughout the year. In forested regions where winter temperatures are cold and the growing season is relatively short, coniferous evergreen forests usually dominate. Deciduous forests with trees that lose their leaves in winter are usually found in regions with milder winters and longer growing seasons. It is obvious to anyone who has seen these two types of forest that the light conditions are dramatically different, as are the wildflowers. While the deciduous forest may cast dense shade during

The floor of a coniferous forest (left) is shady year-round and wildflowers only grow in sunlit gaps. Prairies receive less rainfall than woodlands and contain a diversity of grasses, some shrubs, and wildflowers like Maximilian sunflower (right).

the summer, plenty of light strikes the forest floor in late winter and early spring, and wildflowers proliferate. Coniferous forest, however, casts perpetual shade, and wildflowers tend to grow only in the sunlit gaps where trees have fallen.

Grasslands are found in regions that receive less precipitation than forested areas, and often there are distinct wet and dry seasons, as well as periodic droughts. In North America the transition between forests and prairies begins in the Mississippi River Valley, where annual precipitation is less than about 35 inches. With decreasing amounts of rain and snow, prairie grasses tend to decrease in height, although their roots may penetrate very deeply in search of water. Fire and grazing by large mammals also have played important roles in the maintenance of prairies. Prairies are not just uniform grasses from horizon to horizon; they are extremely diverse plant communities, usually with dozens of different species of perennial (and even some annual) grasses, a great variety of wildflowers, and some shrubs.

Deserts usually receive less than 15 inches of precipitation per year. Like grasslands, they typically have dry and wet seasons, although the

A sunny wetland at the edge of a forest (left) is dominated by handsome plants like cotton grass and cinnamon fern. Even the desert is ablaze in spring with wildflowers, as a field of California poppies blooms near Picacho Peak in Arizona (right).

wet season may not come every year. In North America the major desert regions extend from the Great Basin, between the Sierra Nevada/Cascade Mountains and the Rockies, south into Mexico. The Great Basin deserts have cold winters and are dominated by shrubs like sagebrush, while the warm deserts to the south have mild winters and a greater diversity of shrubs and cacti and other succulents. Periodically, especially during El Niño years, abundant winter precipitation in the desert triggers an amazing display of annual wildflowers in the early spring.

Natural gardeners should take their cue from not only regional vegetation types but also local conditions like topography, drainage, and soil composition. For example, because air temperature decreases as elevation increases, coniferous forests often grow on the higher slopes of mountains in regions that have deciduous forests at lower elevations. Furthermore, at any particular elevation, slopes that face south are sunnier, warmer, and drier than slopes that face north. Slopes that face west are heated by the afternoon sun and therefore tend to be warmer and drier than east-facing slopes. These small differences in topography often lead to large differences in the kinds of vegetation present locally.

Red maple and sugar maple leaves increase soil pH. Choose wildflowers according to your soil conditions.

Topography also influences the drainage conditions at potential garden sites. The tops of hills and ridges tend to have better drainage and drier soils than the bottoms of slopes. Flat areas at the bases of long slopes or near rivers may have sufficient water year-round to support distinctive wetland vegetation. Marshes, dominated by grasses and sedges, and swamps, with shrubs and trees adapted to grow in wet soils, are vital environments that regulate flood water, control pollution, and provide wildlife habitat. While wetland conditions may create challenges for the natural gardener, they also provide opportunities to use the rich palette of species adapted to these habitats.

SIZING UP SOIL

An understanding of your soil is essential for successful wildflower gardening. Soil is not just dirt, but rather a living medium that consists of particles of different sizes, often varying in mineral composition, air spaces, organic matter, moisture, and creatures ranging from bacteria to earthworms. Sandy soils tend to be dry, since they comprise large particles with relatively big spaces in between—conditions that do not retain moisture very well. Soils rich in clay usually drain poorly, as water cannot pass between the tightly packed, microscopic particles. Different wildflowers are adapted to different soil types. The addition of organic matter improves both soil aeration and its ability to retain moisture, although in wetlands an abundance of organic matter can contribute to the mucky soil conditions.

One of the most important soil factors affecting the growth of wildflowers is pH, a measure of relative acidity or alkalinity. On the pH scale, from 0 (most acidic) to 14 (most alkaline), 7 is neutral. The pH of a soil not only results from the chemical composition of the soil minerals, but also is influenced by the decomposition of organic matter, the biological activity of soil organisms, and the chemistry of rain or snow falling on the site. In general, soils that form on top of limestone bedrock are more alkaline and have a higher pH than those formed from granite bedrock.

Many wildflowers survive only within a limited pH range, so you should choose species suited to your soil conditions. Keep in mind that the addition of organic matter such as mulch or compost to wildflower gardens can either raise or lower the pH of the soil, depending on the kind of material added. Pine needles, oak leaves, and peat moss tend to acidify the soil, while the leaves of maples and birches make the soil more alkaline.

THE CONSTANCY OF CHANGE

Plant communities, whether a designed wildflower garden or "natural" vegetation, are constantly changing. Some changes occur on a seasonal or daily basis with various species emerging, flowering, producing fruits, and going into dormancy at different times of the year. In practical gardening terms, this means it is possible to design a wildflower garden with a long season of interest.

Other changes occur over a longer timeline as plant communities respond to disturbances. When a forest is cleared and the land abandoned, it usually does not return immediately to its predisturbance state, but undergoes a gradual recovery through the process of "succession." Fast-growing species with highly mobile seeds are usually the first to arrive. Since many of these species, which we customarily call weeds and pull from our gardens, are short-lived and require lots of sun, they are eventually replaced by less mobile, slower-growing species that are adapted to shade. In other words, in forest regions, open land is first colonized by annual grasses and low-growing plants, then perennial wildflowers and shrubs, and eventually various trees. There may be further changes in the species of trees that dominate the recovering forest, with a shift from the aspens and pines that arrive fairly early to oaks, maples, beech, hemlock, or other species that arrive later, are better adapted to growing in the shade, and live longer. Grasslands and deserts have similar stories to tell, but theirs involve different species in the return to predisturbance conditions.

One of the lessons to be learned from succession is that change is a natural ecological process. A meadow garden in a forested region must be periodically disturbed by fire, weeding, or mowing or it will become a forest. However, a meadow in a grassland region may be more easily maintained, since it resembles the natural vegetation.

When designing your wildflower garden, let nature be your guide. The more observant you are of local environmental conditions, the more successful you will be.

DESIGNING WITH NATURE

by C. Colston Burrell

P ATTERNS ARE COMMON IN NATURE. From the shadows cast by dancing leaves, to ripples in a pond, to overlapping mountain ridges that fade into the haze, natural patterns surround us. In addition to these obvious patterns, there are subtle ones created by the structure of plant communities and the positions plants take in the landscape. Once you understand the factors that create these natural patterns, you can use them to design your wildflower garden.

VERTICAL PATTERNS

Every native plant community, whether forest or grassland, wetland or desert, has a discernible structure based on the dominant and subordinant vegetation. The species in any plant community form vertical layers or strata. A forest has a towering canopy of trees that influences what can and cannot grow beneath it. In a maple-basswood forest, for example, the 30- to 100-foot canopy is high and dense, producing a cathedral-like effect. The canopy is interwoven and connected to form a ceiling over the entire forest. The foliage captures much of the light, protects the forest

Forests have many layers, including trees that form a ceiling beneath taller canopy trees.

interior from rapid temperature fluctuations, and cools the air through evapotranspiration.

Smaller trees such as dogwoods and shadblows make up the airy understory. Understory trees from 30 to 12 feet tall form a more intimate ceiling. Beneath these trees is the shrub layer, between 12 and three feet above the ground, in scattered patches where light and space are sufficient. The shrub layer is a critical foraging and nesting area for a variety of forest birds. Below the shrubs is the ground layer of wildflowers, grasses, sedges, and ferns. Here, spring ephemerals such as spring-beauty bloom first, followed by taller ferns and persistent species like merrybells.

The age of a plant community affects its distribution, composition, and structure. A young forest often has a well-defined shrub layer and understory. Older forests with dense, closed canopies may have fewer ephemeral plants and more persistent or evergreen wildflowers and ferns. The structure of a forest also varies according to the tree species present. Deciduous forests have the most traditional structure, as described above. By comparison, in a dense woodland of coniferous trees, the understory is very thin, but there is often a thick shrub layer, with herbs and mosses carpeting the ground. Coniferous forests have more open canopies, with scattered understory trees and the well-defined shrub layer. Shrub communities have mixed layers of different-sized shrubs, with a ground layer of herbs, grasses, and sedges.

In meadows, prairies, and other communities dominated by herbaceous plants, the vertical structure is no less distinct. However, unlike the trees and shrubs in forests, the plants must resprout from their roots

The patterns of a prairie landscape, dominated by grasses and herbs, can be recreated in a garden. A mini-meadow blankets a sunny backyard with dazzling wildflowers like purple coneflower and black-eyed Susan.

each year. The earliest plants to emerge in the spring, such as violets, are short. Each successive wave of plants to emerge overtops the next, culminating with the tallest grasses and late-blooming composites, such as sunflowers and asters.

HORIZONTAL PATTERNS

Plants within a given community are also distributed in horizontal patterns on the landscape as a result of environmental factors such as soil, moisture, and light. Different species thrive with various amounts of moisture. In a prairie, shrubs grow in the wettest areas, whereas grasses and herbs grow in the slightly higher and drier areas. On ridges, species of smaller stature that cannot compete with the taller lowland vegetation dominate.

In deciduous forests, the dry, sunny ridges support oaks and hickories, while maple and basswood grow in the moister coves in loamy soil on east and north slopes. Individual trees are spaced according to their canopy size and shape. Between the trees, shrubs may abound or be absent. The distribution of species in the ground layer is dependent on

Tree trunks naturally dominate the design of a woodland garden. Native wild-flowers, such as Rocky Mountain columbine, can be used to brighten the ground layer in a garden where deciduous trees cast shade during part of the year.

subtle changes in light, slope, elevation, exposure, and soil moisture. In wetlands, sedges dominate the wettest areas, shrubs the intermediate regions, and prairie or woodland plants the drier uplands. Each species occupies its own niche within the community.

THE BIG PICTURE

To reap maximum ecological benefits, think of your garden as part of a landscape matrix that connects your yard with your neighbors', one neighborhood with another, and your town with the surrounding countryside. Visualize this matrix as an interconnected web and you can see how each home's landscape has a profound influence on the rest of the natural community.

Within your yard you can create a garden in harmony with its surroundings to keep the matrix intact. Locate lawns close to the house, and plant an area of turf no larger than the space you need for family barbecues or summer games of croquet. This is the part of your yard that will be highest in maintenance and lowest in diversity of plants and associated wildlife. Create a shallow depression where water can infiltrate instead of running off of lawns and paths and eventually into nearby waterways, where it can cause erosion and pollution. Also place ornamental and vegetable gardens near the house, perhaps bordering the lawn; consider confining non-native plants to this portion of the garden. If your lot is large, with more space than you need for gardening and recreation, consider a small-scale restoration of the native habitat. You may choose a meadow, prairie, or woodland, based on existing conditions and your region of the country. When linked with wildflower gardens in neighboring yards, these can help reconnect the matrix so that plants and animals aren't trapped in isolated islands in a vast urban or suburban sea.

Next consider the planting design. To start, it helps to visualize a favorite place in the woods or fields and sketch the scene, trying to capture something of the visual quality of the place. If the special place is a woodland, tree trunks will no doubt dominate the picture. In a prairie or meadow, the sea of grasses or scattered clumps of shrubs will create the scene. This exercise will reveal the major structural components and types of plants that give a place its unique character. Understanding this character is fundamental to designing with nature.

To recreate a natural scene in your garden, you must first duplicate or approximate the visual-essence species—those plants that are present in the greatest numbers or that dominate the vertical structure of the plant community. In a woodland it is the tall, dark trunks of trees, those species without which you would not have the woods. To maximize the ecological complexity of your wildflower garden, you must duplicate this vertical structure. Layering adds visual as well as ecological complexity. The canopy creates a monumental feeling. The understory brings the enclosure down to an intimate level, like the ceiling of a living room. Shrubs divide spaces, screen views, and create enclosures. The ground layer, like the furnishings of a room, offers the variety and seasonal interest that all keen gardeners crave.

In a garden modeled on a grassland, tall grasses can take the place of shrubs. These grasses and tall, herbaceous wildflowers are like translucent screens, whereas dense wildflowers, such as cup plants and Joe-pye weed, form solid walls in summer that become see-through in winter.

The wildflower garden does not have to be a reconstruction of nature, however. The design may be highly ordered. A pergola can substitute for tree trunks, with vines forming the canopy. Hedges can be the shrub layer. The point is to represent nature in a form that reflects your individual aesthetic but still functions ecologically.

PORTFOLIO

OF

WILDFLOWER

GARDENS

BEDS AND BORDERS

by Kim Hawks

Beds and borders liberated me as a gardener, transforming my yard into a garden filled with a diversity of plants. Within my beds grow trees, shrubs, herbs, and perennials—including many native North American wildflowers. I plant annuals only sparingly.

My goal for the garden was an informal style—almost a wild look. I have learned from observing nature's gardens that plants grow in layers and have adopted this look in my garden. Spring ephemerals are followed by summer herbaceous plants, overlaid with a loose canopy of shrubs and small trees. I've also learned that in the wild, bare ground always begs to be filled. Plants like to be in the company of other plants, rather than having neat, barren spaces between them; so, I use the recommended spacing for each plant and intersperse annual or biennial natives in bare areas. Encouraging wildlife in the garden, especially butterflies, birds, and dragonflies, was important, too. I also wanted to reduce my acre or so of turf to a much smaller area. All of these goals were achieved when I began creating borders and free-form island beds.

One way to unify such a garden is to design walkways and beds simultaneously; a path emerges and each bed begins to relate to the others. Another way I tie together my garden is by randomly repeating certain plants throughout all the beds. These "signature" plants draw the eye from one bed to the next and create a unifying whole. Examples in my garden include purple verbena, switch-grass, and artemisia.

ADDING WILDFLOWERS

I enjoy bringing wild plants into the garden. Although the bottom line for me is not a plant's origins but whether it has what I'm looking for (purple flowers, say, or nectar for butterflies), my selection often turns out to be a North American native.

The differences between using native or more traditional, exotic perennials are minimal but merit discussion. Some gardening books advise us to feed perennials regularly, or at least to amend the soil at planting time with organic matter, including copious amounts of manure. However, if you pre-

Wildflower beds and borders, unified by paths and the repetition of plants throughout the garden, support a diversity of plant and animal life.

pare an overly rich soil, many sun-loving native perennials become lush monsters and outgrow themselves. Some gardeners believe that native perennials do not require any soil preparation or other coddling. The truth lies somewhere between overindulgence and neglect. Always start by selecting a plant that will thrive in your existing soil. If you are planting a native perennial that was propagated in a nursery, most likely it has been grown in a soilless medium. It hasn't experienced the soils of local fields or roadsides, so it needs assistance getting estab-

lished. Plant your new native in a loosened soil amended with organic matter and mulch, and water it regularly until it becomes established.

I've also discovered that many wildflowers indigenous to wet areas tolerate slightly drier sites in cultivation. For instance, Joe-pye weed inhabits sunny, wet ditches. Yet it thrives in my garden in a sunny, well-drained area that receives supplemental watering in dry times. However, the reverse is not true: Plants that inhabit dry, lean locations do not like soggy soils.

A striking combination: winecups and Texas bluebonnet.

MIXING UP THE PLANTING

Unless its defining characteristic is its smallness, a border made up exclusively of perennials is the highest-maintenance area of the garden. For this reason, in my borders and island beds I incorporate compact or dwarf shrubs, small ornamental trees, and vines (I let them scramble up the shrubs and trees). Woody plants also offer color in their foliage, fruits, and flowers. American beautyberry, for example, has striking purple berries, like amethyst jewels, that spiral around the stems in whorls of color. Small to medium native ornamental trees include snowbell, redbud, and pink flowering dogwood.

Draw attention to your beds and borders by combining plants with sharply different foliage, texture, or form. Keep the composition slightly off balance by using some plants in large numbers and others in arrangements of one or three. For example, switch-grass has a loose, vertical structure to four or five feet, and in the fall its showy seed heads add an airy quality. Combine this native grass with the bold, six- to seven-foot-tall Joe-pye weed, with its rounded mauve flowers, and you've got a striking contrast. To reinforce the vertical lines, add some cabbage-leaf coneflower, with its rockets of black-eyed Susan-like flowers reaching five to six feet. Garden phlox repeats the rounded form of Joe-pye weed in miniature, topping out at four feet, and blooms three to four weeks before it, along with four-foot purple coneflower. Southern blue flag iris rounds out this composition with its boldly vertical, four-foot-high foliage and violet-blue, yellow-splotched flowers.

I place fragrant plants near the edge of the beds where they can be enjoyed. I also plant white flowers or variegated plants along the edges to illuminate the paths in the evening. Great wildflowers to light the way include the early summer-flowering white garden phlox and dwarf fothergilla, which offers numerous white bottle-brush-like flowers early in the season. Mountain mints offer cool, silvery foliage—deliciously fragrant when touched—amid tiered, usually white (depending on the species) flowers.

WILDFLOWERS AND WILDLIFE

One of my favorite island beds has a meadow theme and is home to native wildflowers that grow five to eight feet tall. Here I have learned how to garden with aggressive plants, placing "aggressives with aggressives" and letting them work out their own balance. Wildflowers in this bed include Joe-pye weed, cabbage-leaf coneflower, various powdery mildew-resistant bee balms, mountain mints, and goldenrods.

My entire garden is planted with wildflowers for butterflies, which naturally flock to these dependable, nectar-rich natives. Plant a wide diversity of native wildflowers to provide nectar throughout the seasons. Native sunflowers, coneflowers, butterfly weed, black-eyed Susans, blazing stars, asters, and Joe-pye weed are among the wildflowers that offer plentiful nectar.

Resist the temptation to cut back flowering stems the moment

Combine plants of different forms.

the blossoms wilt and you will be rewarded with your own "living birdseed" feeders. Birds are particularly attracted to the seeds of asters, black-eyed Susans, coreopsis, blazing stars, and goldenrods. When seed heads disperse, however, you may end up with unwanted seedlings. Scratch them out early and the task will not seem overwhelming.

Layers of native wildflowers enhance garden beds and borders. Your yard will not only be more beautiful, but also will celebrate your particular region—whether it is the mountains, the desert, the plains, or, as in my case, the Piedmont.

SHADE GARDENS

SHADE GARDENS

by Carole Ottesen

As a rule, gardeners don't seek out shade. Eventually and inevitably, shade happens. Slim saplings grow stout, casting ever-larger, leafy patterns over lawn and border. Suddenly, one fine day there it is: The yard is all shade. Tomatoes and zinnias are no longer possibilities. However, this new reality makes it possible to embark on one of gardening's most gratifying adventures: A wildflower garden in the shade. The best model for the design of such a garden is a native woodland.

LAYING THE GROUNDWORK

The connection between forest and shade garden is more than merely visual. Processes that occur in a woodland are the same ones at work in a shaded yard. In a woodland, leaves, plant litter, twigs, and branches decompose slowly into humus that builds up the friable, deep, moisture-retentive soil favored by forest plants.

To recreate this rich-soil environment in a garden, you can gather the leaves, branches, and litter to compost them before top-dressing garden beds—a labor-intensive project that has the advantage of looking neat. The alternative is to practice a modified kind of "sheet composting"—allowing litter to decompose in place, made neat looking, if necessary, with a cover of mulch or chopped leaves. Sheet-composting is a good way to make a garden bed out of a lawn area that no longer receives enough sun to support lush grass. Several inches of leaf litter covering the prospective bed in fall will kill the grass beneath. In warm spells throughout the fall, winter, and early spring, the pile of organic matter will decompose, beginning the transformation of ordinary garden soil into something more like the humus-rich soil of a woodland. Earthworms help the process along, enriching the soil with their castings.

SHADES OF SHADE

Plants in a woodland layer themselves as they compete for light—from the tops of forest trees, to understory trees, down to shrubs and herbaceous plants. In the shade garden, it makes sense to group plants accordingly, where light is most abundant. When herbaceous wildflowers are placed with understory trees and

In a shady garden, wildflowers such as woodland phlox, foamflower, and Solomon's seal fringe a meandering path.

Subdued light accents the discreet texture and hues of unfurling bloodroot.

shrubs on the bright side of large trees, and in a fringe along path openings, the result looks spontaneous and natural.

The choice of plants for the shady wildflower garden is limited only by the amount of light or lack of it. Most shade gardens possess a range of light intensity, from "part shade"—just a hair too shady to grow sun-loving plants—to "deep shade"—a darkish place that doesn't receive any direct sunlight. In between these extremes is "medium shade," sometimes described as "dappled shade," where the sun filters teasingly through moving leaves of the tree canopy, or "high shade," a place with bright light but no direct sun. Summer, when the tree canopy is at its fullest, is the best time to map out a garden's degrees of shade and select corresponding plants for each area.

Short of felling, limbing up trees is the classic method of increasing light in a woodland. Gardeners do this to achieve "part shade," with its wide realm of potential plant inhabitants. Because most plants tolerate a range of light conditions, virtually all shade-loving plants and quite a few sun-lovers will grow and thrive in part shade.

SHADY CHARACTERS

Fortunately, there is no dearth of shade-loving plants to occupy parts of the garden in medium to deep shade. Spring ephemerals such as Virginia bluebell and trilliums thrive in any part of a shady garden, because they receive all the light they need in early spring before the trees leaf out. By late spring when the tree canopy fills out, they die down, completing the active part of their life cycle before going dormant in summer. Along with the wood phloxes, ephemerals provide the earliest color and interest. Later arrivals such as baneberry and bottle gentian can be planted beside ephemerals so that when they die down, their spaces will be filled with plants that carry on until fall.

For new gardens, some of the most versatile and forgiving plants are wood poppy, wild geranium, and wild gingers. They tolerate a range of conditions and establish quickly. Eventually, wild geranium, wild ginger, and wood poppy will spread into seamless groundcovers that discourage weeds. Massed in groundcover, these plants provide rich texture—a valuable commodity in any garden but especially welcome and fitting in a shady one. Subdued light renders a shady garden serene; in its peaceful atmosphere, subtleties like the patterns and rhythms of texture become dominant features.

Likewise, in the shade, a little color goes a long way. While gentle light accentuates the contrasts and nuances among the greens, the bold-colored plants that thrive in sunny gardens may appear jarringly out of place in the shade. Appropriately, many of the perennials for shade are discreetly hued. In spring, a shady garden is alight with the blues of dwarf crested iris, Virginia bluebell, and Jacob's ladder, and the whites of the great white trillium, baneberries, and bloodroot.

Adding summer color to the shady garden requires a bit more guile. One small break in the tree canopy, natural or fabricated, will admit shafts of sunlight that will support one or two vibrantly hued plants. A hot spot of red in a sea of greens makes up in intensity for what is not possible in number. Cardinal flower, which holds its scarlet blooms aloft in late summer, is an excellent candidate for this role. Red- or fuchsia-colored bee balm work equally well.

Gardening in the shade is different from gardening in full sun. It is cooler and more comfortable. It is accomplished only in full cooperation with nature and a watchful eye on the tree canopy. It is limited to a small but exceedingly choice coterie of plants. Finally, while it has its share of challenges, it has more than its share of rewards.

WATER AND BOG GARDENS

by Madeleine Keeve

WATER AND
BOG GARDENS

Water is H$_2$O, hydrogen two parts, oxygen one, but there is also a third thing that makes it water, and nobody knows what this is.
—D.H. Lawrence, "The Third Thing," *Pansies*, 1929

Just as a good gardener reveres soil as an integral part of a garden's complicated existence, so a good pondkeeper appreciates a body of water as an active ecosystem that supports all manner of organisms—not just plants. Unlike a swimming pool, a water garden teems with life.

If you have a pond, a stream, or a boggy area on your property, you have a special opportunity to create a garden habitat that works with nature. You control the design of a water garden, but the control is actually a kind of stewardship, an appreciation of what nature can do better than any gardener. The only rule is: Use plants suited to your water environment and the garden will thrive.

AQUATIC AND BOG PLANTS

Aquatic plants, such as water-lilies and pickerel weed, that grow in still water, and bog plants, such as marsh mallow, which grow in water-logged soil, are easy to cultivate, once you become familiar with their native habitats and locate them in suitable areas of the garden. Open areas in full sun are the natural habitats for many aquatic and bog plants. However, while few true aquatics do well in shade, many bog plants thrive there.

Light exposure isn't the only consideration when choosing plants for the garden. Different watery conditions also present various opportunities for a range of plants. Aquatics flourish in the placid waters of a pool or pond. The moving water of a stream can't sustain aquatics, but it can support rich plant growth along its banks. The constant presence of moisture on the shady edge of a stream allows you to grow many ferns and wildflowers, including lobelias and foamflowers, as well as shrubs such as winterberry, red-twig dogwood, and swamp azalea. A naturally wet area in your garden, such as a spring-fed ditch or a low-lying area with poor drainage, is a perfect spot for some North American native iris or the curious woodlander, Jack-in-the-pulpit.

Umbrella leaf flourishes on the banks of a stream of rushing water.

When choosing plants for a water or bog garden, it is also necessary to acquaint yourself with the soil at the site: Is it sandy, heavy clay, or rock-filled? Do the edges stay dry or waterlogged all season? Does your boggy area go bone dry in August? Such factors will determine which plants are most suitable for the particular conditions.

Be sure to learn all about the plants you'd like to cultivate: their native range, hardiness, ultimate size, how quickly they grow and multiply, whether or not they attract birds or insects. Many plants are polite growers, or easily restrained, but some, such as horsetail (*Equisetum fluviatile*) may be aggressive or even invasive in your area, even if they are native to North America. Consult local experts to make sure that any plant you introduce in your water garden will not escape into nearby natural areas and become a pest.

DESIGN CONSIDERATIONS

The constant presence of water allows aquatic and bog plants to produce lush foliage with well-defined shapes, and often a reflective, water-repellent sheen. Choose these plants on the merits

The bold color and striking leaves of blue flag iris help to anchor a pond.

of their leaves as well as their flowers, which come and go quickly. Water-lilies, skunk cabbage, and hardy water canna (*Thalia dealbata*), among many others, have large, beautifully shaped leaves with a bold, almost tropical presence that provide interest even when the plants are out of flower.

When it comes to plants in a pond or bog, fewer is better. The ecology of a healthy pond or pool requires that roughly one-third to one-quarter of the water's surface remains free of plant cover. While that may seem like an awful lot of open space, remember that a body of still water is a flat, shining surface, reflecting the sky and surrounding vegetation. Be sure to keep this in mind when designing your water garden. Any reflective surface, whether water or mirror, makes everything look larger, and so each plant in a pond or pool will appear to be doubled in size.

Even in a small space, however, locate at least one large plant with a strong presence, such as the native umbrella leaf (*Diphylleia cymosa*), in or near the water. One or two large plants allied with a few smaller companions creates a more pleasing effect than a variety of small plants—they will only look chaotic, and make no impression when viewed from a distance.

When combining water and/or bog plants, don't think of them as individual specimens but rather as communities: shade-tolerant plants belong in one area, and sun-lovers in another. Then, within each area or community, combine plants with an eye toward interesting combinations of size, leaf shape, color, and texture. For example, the majestic leaves of western skunk cabbage might dominate a boggy area; smaller companions with markedly different leaves such as marsh marigold and bellwort would be good companions—all are tolerant of partial shade and flower in early spring. Each plant in the threesome contributes leaves and flowers of different sizes and shapes, but the flowers of all three are shades of yellow, unifying the composition.

While the plants are still in containers, don't hesitate to experiment with their placement. You might even set the pots in a test arrangement, leave them for a while, then return at another time of day or view them from another direction to see if the combination still pleases you.

As in any naturalistic garden, the great constant in the water

Marsh marigold's bright color lights up wet sites in partial shade.

garden is change: The amount of light changes with the seasons, temperatures rise and fall, and plants emerge, flower, and die back. Learn to work with these changes to foster an environment you will treasure in all seasons. You'll enjoy not only the plants you've arranged, but also the dynamics of a thriving ecosystem—fish jumping up to catch mosquitos, dragonflies and birds looking for landing sites, frogs croaking love songs at dusk. If D.H. Lawrence had been a water gardener, he'd have recognized, in the hullabaloo, that third thing.

MEADOW AND PRAIRIE GARDENS

by Joan Feely

It's a late June day, and the coneflowers, Culver's root, and spiderworts are in their glory. The seed heads of the cool-season grasses are backlit by the setting sun, as they sway in the warm breeze. As you walk along your meadow path, butterflies abandon their flowers to seek out the salty perspiration on your brow, American goldfinches scatter at your approach, and the kids race ahead to find the box turtle that they glimpsed the day before.

With their promise of just this sort of scene, meadows and prairies have inspired a new and appealing garden style. Gardens modeled on meadows and their closely related Midwestern counterparts, prairies, are truly minimal-maintenance landscapes, less polluting than the high-care lawns they often replace, yet retaining the openness of manicured turf. The diverse plant life of these wildflower-filled grasslands supports a wide array of animal life. And this wildlife is not in the treetops or out in the middle of a pond. It is close at hand, flying about at eye level, and scurrying around the next sunflower.

Lady Bird Johnson's efforts to reintroduce bluebonnet and Indian paintbrush to the Texas roadsides have inspired gardeners across America. Unfortunately, the annuals that make the Texas roadsides so beautiful are native to that state and do not grow well in other parts of the United States. In order to recreate the colorful displays along the Texas roadsides in places such as North Carolina, Maryland, and Ohio, landscape designers often rely on annuals and biennials from Europe and California. This has led to the birth of the "instant meadow." These artificial meadows have little wildlife value, must be replaced each year, and require more work than a perennial bed. In the Midwest and East at least, the showy wildflowers are perennials, not annuals and biennials as they are in the arid West.

You need to look locally for the natural model and the appropriate plants for your grassland garden. Every region in the United States has splendid, natural meadow-like habitats dominated by grasses and adorned with wildflowers of every description, from delicate lilies to

In its second year, a beautiful meadow planting of native wildflowers in Iowa has come into its own and needs little maintenance or extra water.

monstrously tough and tall rosin-weed (growing to 12 feet in moist prairies!). Any garden can include a meadow component, whether it be a sidewalk strip for a city garden or a multi-acre swath on a sprawling property.

MEADOW DESIGN

Designing a meadow is much like designing any garden. The first order of business is deciding where it is going to go. The site must have at least eight hours of direct sun. Soils that are not overly fertile produce the best results, as they support fewer weeds.

When selecting species to include in your meadow, start with dessert—the wildflowers. Think in terms of choosing plants suited to your topography and soil, as well as the individual wildflower's season of bloom; after the meadow is established, watering, pruning, and deadheading should be unnecessary. Buy your plants and seeds from nurseries close to home, which should have the species most adapted to your environmental conditions.

It's helpful to create a base map that delineates the topographic variation and the soil moisture levels of your site. Using a set of four or five transparencies that overlay one another will help you visualize the seasons of bloom. Make separate sheets for spring, early summer, high summer, fall, and winter.

Aim for 20 to 30 wildflower species. To achieve a natural look, keep in mind that in natural prairies and meadows, the dominant wildflowers are daisy relatives such as asters, coneflowers, sunflowers, and goldenrods. Legumes make up the next largest group, including the indigos, native clovers, partridge pea, and wild lupine. In moisture-retentive soils, bee balm and spiderwort will thrive, along with queen-of-the-prairie and giant meadow rue. Don't forget the milkweeds (*Asclepias* species), which are essential to the monarch butterfly's life cycle.

The grasses in your meadow or prairie garden set it apart from the traditional perennial garden. They can be divided into two simple categories: tall and short. Generally, the taller grasses prefer moderately moist soils; the shorter grasses, drier soils. Place the tallest grasses—big bluestem, Indian grass, purple top, and eastern gama grass—toward the center or rear of the garden. Smaller grasses such as little bluestem, broom sedge, purple lovegrass, and prairie dropseed accent the showy wildflowers.

There are two basic approaches to arranging meadow plants. Scattering the different species through-

In areas where homeowners have traditional turf lawns, it helps to keep the peace among neighbors by mowing the edges of a wildflower meadow.

out the site will create a fine-textured garden that invites closer inspection, but be sure to sprinkle together species that bloom at the same time for the best show. Another approach is to group species in masses, providing splashes of color for your pleasure—and easy targets for nectar-seeking hummingbirds and butterflies.

When designing a meadow garden, it is important to create a sense of intent. A rustic fence along the perimeter, a cleanly mown edge, or a beautiful sculpture announces to the neighbors that someone is caring for the garden, that in this place something enticing is going to happen.

HOW-TO'S

You must control the undesirable plants at the site before planting a meadow garden. Planting directly into sods of Kentucky bluegrass or zoysia will not result in a thriving garden, and overseeding turf will result in total failure. Only in a lawn of native grasses should you plant into existing turf.

If a pampered lawn is to be converted to meadow, a year of

Purple coneflower and prairie clover are lovely prairie wildflowers.

growing the lawn with no fertilizer while continuing to mow will help use up the excess nutrients that benefit weeds more than desired wildflowers. Methods for clearing the ground include covering smaller areas with black plastic, applying herbicides, and using a sod cutter. The first two methods require a full year of treatment to control both cool- and warm-season plants.

A meadow garden can be started with seed, plants, or a combination of both, depending on your budget and how long you can wait for your meadow garden to bloom. Wildflowers planted from seed will bloom after three years. A small number of native bienni-als such as black-eyed Susan can be included in the seed mix to color up the first years. If weeds are a problem, cut the meadow at six inches; this will not harm the young seedlings, but will reduce weed seed production. Sowing grass seed in late spring or early summer and adding wildflower plants in the fall will result in a mature meadow in less time. Using only plants is most affordable on smaller sites.

Once the meadow takes hold, basic maintenance consists of an annual mowing, done in the winter, if possible. If your meadow backs up to a woodland, special attention must be paid to the woodland edge, because birds perched there will plant various fleshy-fruited species, such as Japanese honeysuckle, bittersweet, and mulberry, to name a few. Remove these weedy species as soon as possible, as they have the potential to overrun your grassland.

When you create a meadow, you are creating the most basic sustainable landscape. Nature will have an important role to play, determining in large part the ultimate density of your wildflowers, the lushness of your grasses, the height of your Joe-pye weed. As many a gardener has discovered, a meadow or prairie garden is a true partnership with nature.

Wildflower species like butterfly weed grown in masses provide splashes of color and easy targets for butterflies, such as this fritillary.

HELL STRIPS AND ROCKERIES

by James Stevenson

Rushing in to create a garden where angels fear to tread may seem like a foolish endeavor, but to the plant enthusiast, no patch of ground can be left untouched. Such is the case with the hell strip—an area that is inaccessible to regular maintenance, has poor soil, or is exposed to heat, cold, punishing wind, or any other extreme condition.

A hell strip could be the area between the sidewalk and the road, along a fence outside your garden, or between the parking lot and the garage. It could be an island surrounded by pavement, a ditch, or a berm—anywhere attempts to beautify are defeated by the site's unpleasantness. Or perhaps your hell strip is a "rockery"—a pile of concrete or bricks from a past project, or a natural outcropping.

Most gardeners clothe their hell strips in turf and maintain them with the mower, or plant a bank of low-maintenance groundcover. However, if it is highly visible, a bit of inspired design can dress up your hell strip. And if you really think it through and make careful plant choices, you can have a garden area that requires little maintenance.

LOOK TO NATURE

Rather than trying to "fight the site" with costly manipulation of soil and water conditions, plant your hell strip with species suited to the existing conditions. Base your plant selections on the native plant communities that grow on similar sites. Just because black-eyed Susan is native to your area doesn't mean that it will thrive in the shaded muck in your backyard; its native habitat is poor soils in full sun. Look instead to the plant communities in your region that grow naturally in mucky, shaded places.

I have even drawn inspiration from gas stations and fast food restaurants for plants that will withstand extreme conditions. Though no one tends these plants, they manage to thrive and color the landscape (often matching the lurid colors of the business sign). For example, the thread-leaf yucca (*Yucca filamentosa*) always seems thrilled to rise up out of burgundy-colored pumice mulch. Think of incorporating the survivors you find in your area with tough-as-nails native wildflowers and non-native perennials for a mixed planting

Moss phlox is a low-growing wildflower that makes an excellent lawn alternative or beautifies a rocky site where other plants might languish.

ready to take on the elements. Combining tough woody plants with seasonally showy wildflowers and perennials can create an enviable display with a modicum of maintenance.

Part of the fun is deciding what effect you want to create throughout the year. Perhaps you want a big, audacious bounty of bloom all summer long, doubling as a screen or barrier. Large wildflowers and grasses suit this design well, and the grasses such as panic grass (*Panicum virgatum*) remain upright and create a

screen through the winter as well. Or maybe you want a lawn alternative with short flowering plants. In this case, moss phlox, poppy mallows, sundrops, and native sedums and wallflowers are a few plants to consider.

Hell strips call for perennials that can take abuse, such as indigos and lupines with dramatic spires of blue, white, or yellow flowers and a lovely spherical outline of foliage the rest of the year. A choice cultivar, *Baptisia* × 'Purple Smoke', combines the charcoal stems of the white-flowering

Purple coneflower (left) lures butterflies to sites where many plants fear to tread. White wild indigo (right) also withstands extreme conditions.

species with the blue-violet flowers of wild blue indigo.

Among the early-flowering perennials you may wish to interplant specimens whose foliage holds down the fort all year round. Tough types like the native prairie sage (*Artemisia ludoviciana*) lend foliar interest between floral displays. Other foliage plants include the ornamental grasses—they are perfectly suited to extreme environments. Large species, such as the upright panic grass, are best relegated to the back of a planting.

In summer, a plethora of wonderful wildflowers reigns. Purple coneflowers provide great garden presence as well as a wealth of nectar for butterflies. Black-eyed Susan can certainly stand its ground in a hell strip, combining well with the creeping North American native *Verbena canadensis*, which creates a hazy purple groundcover all summer long. The cabbage-leafed coneflower towers in bloom to seven or eight feet. The flower's central black cone is set off by the drooping, cheerful golden yellow petals, but

Grasses like panic grass grow dense and tall in inhospitable areas of the garden, providing color and texture and acting as a screen all summer.

its wide blue-gray foliage is reason enough to grow it.

Fall belongs to the asters and goldenrods. Asters come in a range of colors, all harmonious in the slanting rays of sunlight at the end of the year. Goldenrods have long been blamed for causing hay fever, but this is not so. What they do cause is "oohs" and "aahs" when the burst of golden flowers arrives on the scene.

ROOTING AROUND A ROCKERY

Like the hell strip, a rockery is a challenging and fun site to gussy up. It may be a ruin of rubble or rocks, or a stacked-stone retaining wall, complete with nooks and crannies perfect for tucking in little plant treasures.

Choosing plants for my own sunny rockery was easy. I am a rabid crocophile, and I planted as many of the little species crocuses as I could get my hands on. Instead of planting them in drifts, I planted pockets of five or so bulbs in the spaces between rocks and around the base. Many traditional rock garden plants suffer in our humid North

Carolina summers, so to a great extent I turned once again to the native plant communities to search for those adapted to our climate. Locating a nursery source for one of my favorite spring flowers, bluet (*Houstonia serpyllifolia*), was a happy day. Bluet creates a spreading mat of foliage festooned with little blue stars in spring and summer and does not go dormant but rather persists as a foliage plant when out of bloom. Stargrass (*Hypoxis hirsuta*) blooms in early summer with cheerful yellow stars on slender stems. Though stargrass is found in the woods and in edge situations, it seems happy out in the sun.

If I weren't moving this year, I'd add an extraordinary little native American perennial bluestar (*Amsonia tenuifolia* var. *filifolia*). It looks like Easter-basket grass that has blown into the garden, as its incredibly fine-textured, light green foliage froths out of the rocks. In spring, light blue star-shaped flowers are displayed at the tips of the wiry stems. Contrasting the bluestar yet remaining in the same scale is another native, green and gold (*Chrysogonum virginianum*), with paddle-shaped, dark green leaves and one- to two-inch gold flowers. As the beauty of its display peaks in April, green and gold is not particularly long-lived, but it does grow rapidly.

A wall can be a fun place to situate plants that will reseed themselves into the crevices. I have seen *Corydalis* species appear clinging to a vertical slope between wall stones. This is due to the fact that their seeds are dispersed by ants, who can navigate this gravitationally tricky terrain. Other ant-dispersed native wildflowers include wild bleeding heart (*Dicentra eximia*) and wakerobin (*Trillium* species).

Perhaps your rockery is located under trees and receives sunlight only during the early months of spring, before the trees leaf out. In summer, competition for soil moisture is fierce, and the large trees inevitably seem to win. Consider, in this case, the spring ephemerals that carpet the forest floor early in the year with a rush of bloom, then quietly slip into dormancy for the rest of the summer. A walk through the woods in early spring reveals a wealth of native treasures such as rue anemone (*Thalictrum thalictroides*), hepaticas, and bloodroot. These plants are often found growing in the thin soil under large and thirsty deciduous trees on dry, south-facing slopes. Add favorite bulbs such as crocus, snowdrop, and cyclamen, and you will have a lovely display.

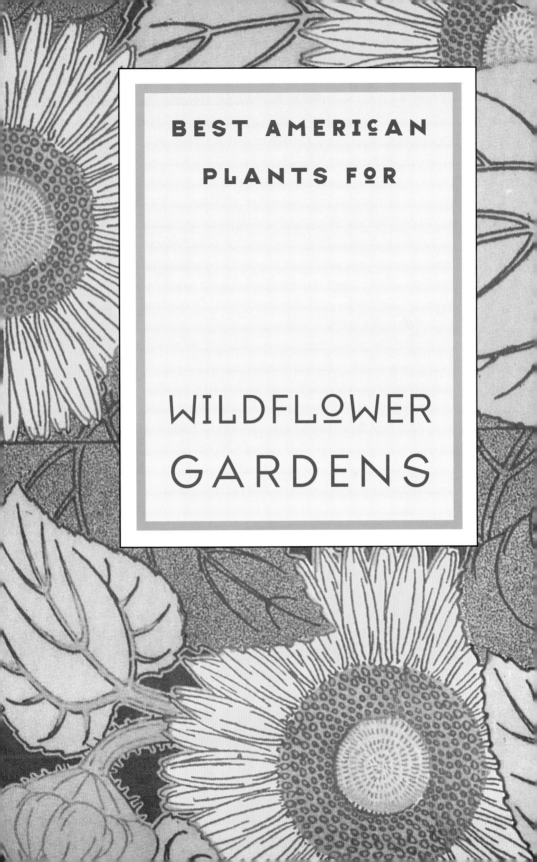

BEST AMERICAN PLANTS FOR

WILDFLOWER GARDENS

SHADE

WILDFLOWERS FOR SHADE

by Carole Ottesen

Actaea pachypoda
WHITE BANEBERRY

White baneberry's April flowers, which look like frothy white balls, are followed in late summer and autumn by showy, black-dotted white berries. These fruits have earned the plant another of its common names, "doll's eyes." Pretty flowers and intriguing berries add to baneberry's charms, but by far its finest attribute is its graceful, lacy foliage, which resembles that of *Cimicifuga* species. Baneberry's superb foliage is, at once, both lush and fine. A boon in the shady garden, it adds freshness and good looks at a time when many early spring bloomers are fading.

White baneberry

Baneberry prefers a slightly acid soil but is otherwise carefree.

NATIVE HABITAT AND RANGE: Woodlands from Nova Scotia, south to Georgia and west to Minnesota and Missouri.

USDA HARDINESS ZONES: 4 to 8

HABIT, USE, AND COMPANIONS: An excellent plant to layer between shrubs and a groundcover such as wild ginger (*Asarum* species), baneberry's handsome 2′ to 3′-tall foliage adds volume and texture as it camouflages the dying leaves of ephemerals such as Virginia bluebells (*Mertensia virginica*).

CULTIVARS AND RELATED SPECIES: The flowers and foliage of red baneberry (*A. rubra*) are similar to white baneberry's, but the fruits that emerge in summer are a bright, cherry red. The berries of both plants—white and red—are poisonous. Found in woodland and thickets from Labrador to Ontario and south to New Jersey, Pennsylvania, Nebraska, and South Dakota. Zones: 4 to 8.

Aralia racemosa
SPIKENARD

Spikenard's foliage is rugged and striking—big and light green with prominently veined, compound leaves. As the plant develops in late spring, there is a sense that something extraordinary is going to happen. Then clusters of quiet and respectable greenish white flowers bloom in early summer, but it isn't until the flowers are followed by stalks of showy purple berries that there is a sense of fulfillment. Spikenard requires shade and moisture and will sulk most unattractively if its needs are not met.

NATIVE HABITAT AND RANGE: Rich woodlands from Maine to Georgia and west to Minnesota, South Dakota, and Missouri, as well as the Rocky Mountains.

USDA HARDINESS ZONES: 3 to 8

HABIT, USE, AND COMPANIONS: Spikenard grows to 3′ tall with an equal spread. Its curiously overlapping leaves suggest a cantilevered structure, an unusual habit that draws attention wherever it is placed. It is a bold plant for the back of a woodland border or layering between shrubs and perennials. It also serves as a small specimen shrub and contrasts well with palm branch sedge (*Carex muskingumensis*), hostas, or ferns.

CULTIVARS AND RELATED SPECIES: Wild sarsaparilla (*A. nudicaulis*) is a daintier species than spikenard, growing to 1′ to 1½′ tall with small, green flowers and a

Spikenard

pungent aroma. Plant in average to rich, moist soil. Zones 3 to 8.

Asarum canadense
WILD GINGER
A fast spreader that becomes dense in shade, wild ginger's wonderfully rounded leaves provide intriguing texture and a finished look along edges and paths. A quart-sized pot of wild ginger, planted in moist shade in spring, will easily cover more than a square foot by fall. The only fault of this excellent groundcover is that it is not evergreen like its less hardy counterpart, western wild ginger (*A. caudatum*).

SHADE

Wild ginger, a fast-spreading groundcover, grows densely in shady gardens.

NATIVE HABITAT AND RANGE: Rich woodlands from New Brunswick to North Carolina, west to Missouri.

USDA HARDINESS ZONES: 3 to 8

HABIT, USE, AND COMPANIONS: Wild gingers are great groundcovers and—because they are shallow-rooted—excellent for keeping weeds away from shrubs without competing themselves. It is easy to remove them from places where they are not wanted. They also transplant easily. Because the plants are low—only 6″ tall—and uniform, they consort beautifully with just about any plant in the garden, but particularly with maidenhair fern (*Adiantum pedatum*), blue phlox (*P. divaricata*), and trilliums.

CULTIVARS AND RELATED SPECIES: Western wild ginger (*A. caudatum*) is sometimes called "long-tailed wild ginger" for the long tails on its flowers. Like the "little brown jug" flowers of *A. canadense*, these are maroon and brown. One has to get to one's knees and look under the foliage to see them, as they rest directly on the ground, hidden under the leaves. Found in rich woodlands from British Columbia to California. Zones 4 to 8.

Asarum arifolium
HEARTLEAF WILD GINGER

Heartleaf wild ginger's glossy, faintly mottled, evergreen leaves are borne on plants that creep outward, but ever so slowly. The plant stays in place, but grows fuller and more handsome with age as each spring a new flush of glossy, bright green leaves appears. For a woodland garden, a groundcover that stays put as this plant does is desirable but hard to find. Lovely and dependable, heartleaf wild ginger is an anchoring plant that frames rambling companions.

NATIVE HABITAT AND RANGE: Rich woodlands from Virginia south to Alabama and Florida.

USDA HARDINESS ZONES: 4 to 9

HABIT, USE, AND COMPANIONS: With medium green, faintly mottled leaves that spread out, vaselike, from a central clump, heartleaf wild ginger is perfect as an edging plant along a path. At 8″ tall, it acts as a handsome frame for companions such as fairy wands (*Chamaelirium luteum*) or the taller trilliums like purple toadshade (*Trillium cuneatum*) and yellow trillium (*T. luteum*).

CULTIVARS AND RELATED SPECIES: Shuttleworth ginger (*A. shuttleworthii*) is also evergreen and roughly similar in appearance, but is not as hardy. It is also far more variable, but if there were an aver-

SHADE

Heartleaf wild ginger is a bright green groundcover that stays put.

SHADE

age Shuttleworth ginger, it would have somewhat rounded, dark green leaves and distinct silver mottling. Variations among the Shuttleworths include wildly mottled gingers, those of more discreet appearance, slow-moving ones, and those that wander ceaselessly. The cultivar 'Callaway', from Callaway Gardens in Georgia, is an especially fine, vigorous ginger with silver mottling. Found in rich woodlands from Virginia south to Georgia and Alabama. Zones 5 to 8.

Astilbe biternata
FALSE GOAT'S BEARD
Big and bold, false goat's beard looks like the giant astilbe that it is. The leaflets of downy green have toothed edges similar to those of the garden variety astilbe—only larger and more rugged looking. Responsive to growing conditions, false goat's beard will reach a height of 5′ and bear leaves measuring as much as 2′ across when grown in the moist, rich soil it prefers.

Rare in the wild, this member of the Saxifrage family is unique in the garden. It can be counted upon to provide volume and fullness in the shade, where these attributes are frequently lacking. In comparison to the flowers of garden astilbes, the blooms of false goat's beard are subdued. In late May and June, pyramid-shaped panicles of small, white, yellowish, or cream flowers appear over the top of the leaves.

NATIVE HABITAT AND RANGE: Rich woodlands from Maryland and Virginia south to Georgia, west to Kentucky.

USDA HARDINESS ZONES: 4 to 8

HABIT, USE, AND COMPANIONS: False goat's beard's grand stature makes it a superb background plant. Strategically planted, a stand of false goat's beard is a cunning way to stop the eye from wandering out of the garden—or to guide it in the desired direction. Used in numbers, this generous plant can also serve as a loose, informal hedge. As a layering plant, false goat's beard is just the right size to step down from tall shrubs or understory trees. One layer below false goat's beard, try goat's beard (*Aruncus dioicus*) and baneberry (*Actaea* species), which have similar foliage. Better yet, contrast the fine-textured leaves with bold plants such as umbrella leaf (*Diphylleia cymosa*) and wild ginger.

CULTIVARS AND RELATED SPECIES: No other native *Astilbes* available.

Geranium maculatum
WILD GERANIUM
Intoxicating after it has been pelted by raindrops and its leaves release their fragrance, wild geranium

Wild geranium has a spicy fragrance, spreads lustily as it crowds out weeds, and tolerates all light conditions, from deep shade to full sun.

ought to be planted where its spicy perfume drifts indoors. Placing a few plants under windows in the dark spaces between house and shrubs would suit this easy-care plant just fine and fill the adjacent rooms with its sweet aroma. This is not to suggest that wild geranium should be hidden from view. Its handsome, mounding leaves are a downy green with a hint of mottling. Vibrant pink flowers, held over the plants, add to its charm.

NATIVE HABITAT AND RANGE: Woodlands and wooded roadsides throughout eastern and central North America.

USDA HARDINESS ZONES: 2 to 8
HABIT, USE, AND COMPANIONS: Growing about 15″ high, wild geranium forms a low, ground-hugging mound of neat, overlapping, deeply incised leaves dotted with bright pink flowers. Planted along edges, wild geranium is reminiscent of a lacy collar. As a groundcover, wild geranium is carefree. It spreads lustily, engulfing shorter weeds. Removal is easy, as wild geranium roots in the top layer of humus and is easier to pull out than it is to transplant. These characteristics make it useful for keeping a garden

Round-lobed hepatica seems to arise from nowhere in early spring.

under control until it is given over to other uses. Wild geranium tolerates virtually any situation from sun to deep shade. It hides the dying after-bloom foliage of bulbs, and combines well with tall perennials and ferns such as ostrich fern (*Matteuccia pennsylvanica* var. *struthiopteris*) and leggy shrubs such as native azaleas.

CULTIVARS AND RELATED SPECIES: 'Alba' is the name given to white and pale pink selections grown from seed. 'Hazel Gallagher' has large, pure white flowers.

Richardson's geranium (*G. richardsonii*) blooms in early to midsummer. Found in open woods, meadows, and prairies in moist soil in western North America. Zones 4 to 8.

Hepatica americana
ROUND-LOBED HEPATICA

Sighting the first round-lobed hepatica is one of the rituals of spring. When the first shy flower doffs its fuzzy flower-bud cap to brave wind and weather, winter is officially over. The small blue flowers, some of the daintiest denizens of dry, acid shade, seem to rise out of nowhere—by the time they bloom, their evergreen leaves have often succumbed and disappeared into the ground-litter of the previous growing season. Sometimes, when the elements have not totally destroyed them, one can see in round-lobed hepatica's old, purple-brown, liver-shaped leaves the reason for .one of its common names, liverwort. After the appearance of flowers— which may be blue, white or, less commonly, pink—new leaves emerge that are also liver-shaped but are a fresh, pale green.

NATIVE HABITAT AND RANGE: Nova Scotia, Ontario, Manitoba, and Alaska, south to Georgia, Arkansas, Minnesota, and Iowa.

USDA HARDINESS ZONES: 3 to 8

HABIT, USE, AND COMPANIONS: At less than 6" tall, tiny round-lobed hepatica, unless one is lucky enough to have dozens, must be viewed up close to be appreciated. At the edge of a path or, if possible, at eye-level in a terraced garden are the perfect places for it. Excellent companions include other diminutive plants: rue anemone (*Thalictrum thalictroides*), bluets (*Hedyotis* species), and ebony spleenwort (*Asplenium platyneuron*).

CULTIVARS AND RELATED SPECIES: Sharplobe hepatica (*H. acutiloba*) closely resembles round-lobed hepatica, but its flowers are a bit larger and its leaf blades are pointed. Sharplobe hepatica also grows in a more nearly neutral soil with a pH of 6 to 7. It is found in calcareous woodlands throughout eastern North America. Zones 3 to 8.

Iris cristata
DWARF CRESTED IRIS

This diminutive crested iris, a true dwarf, makes up for what it lacks in stature by lustily fanning out across the ground to form great colonies of bright green, lance-shaped leaves. In this, it behaves like a true iris. But where the wildly multiplying garden irises are frequently too much of a good thing—no matter how attractive their spiky leaves—the small size of crested iris's leaves make it a welcome wanderer.

Dwarf crested iris

Crested iris is crowned for much too short a time—perhaps a week or so in late April—with exquisitely delicate, purple-blue flowers, crested with orange. Although the flowers are short-lived, if kept moist, the foliage remains through the growing season.

NATIVE HABITAT AND RANGE: Woodlands of Maryland, south to Georgia and west to southern Indiana and Missouri.

USDA HARDINESS ZONES: 3 to 8

HABIT, USE, AND COMPANIONS: Crested iris stands only 6″ tall with its leaves aligned in the direction of the rhizome from which they arise. It serves

SHADE

Twinleaf has lovely seed pods and leaves shaped like angel's wings.

admirably as an edging or a low groundcover. It might also be used in a garden of other miniatures, such as the tiny bluets and the round-leaved violet (*V. rotundifolia*). Other companions of comparable height and contrasting foliage might include creeping phlox (*P. stolonifera*) and wood sorrel (*Oxalis acetosella*).

CULTIVARS AND RELATED SPECIES: 'Abby's Violet' has deep purple-blue flowers. 'Shenandoah Skies' has rich, sky blue flowers. 'Summer Storm' has deep blue flowers. There is a white-flowered crested iris, *I. cristata alba.*

Jeffersonia diphylla
TWINLEAF

Too rarely seen in gardens, twinleaf bears starry white flowers that resemble those of bloodroot. One inch across and borne singly on 8″ stems, the flowers bloom in late April. As pretty as the blossoms are, twinleaf is far more memorable for its unusual leaves. Absolutely unique, these are carried one to a stem with each leaf cleft very nearly in two. Their mirror-image halves give the impression of flat green butterflies or angel wings. When the wind blows them around, they look like little flags. Their stems continue to grow taller after the flowers fade until they reach about 15". When the seed pods form, they are as unique as the curious leaves. Shaped like tiny tobacco pipes, they have little hinged lids that open when the seeds are ripe.

NATIVE HABITAT AND RANGE: Damp, open woods from Ontario south to Virginia, west to Tennessee, Wisconsin, and Iowa.

USDA HARDINESS ZONES: 3 to 7

HABIT, USE, AND COMPANIONS: Because twinleaf's leaves and flowers rise directly from the rootstock, its habit is loose and open, lending it a rather delicate appearance. This looseness is enhanced after flowering, as the stems continue to grow until they mature at about 15". Not bothered by insects and seemingly impervious to disease, twinleaf thrives in slightly acid, moist soil. It is an intriguing addition to a woodland border. Its stature and loose habit make it perfect for a position slightly off a path, perhaps behind a patch of creeping phlox or the taller blue phlox (*P. divaricata*). Planted with Allegheny spurge (*Pachysandra procumbens*), twinleaf would bloom and rise up over Allegheny spurge before it puts outs its new leaves.

CULTIVARS AND RELATED SPECIES: None available.

Virginia bluebells

Mertensia virginica
VIRGINIA BLUEBELLS

Virginia bluebells grow with wild abandon, popping up everywhere in shady gardens, providing armloads of flowers for picking. Virginia bluebells have been known to spread into dense carpets in the dankest, deepest shade.

The flowers are powder-blue with just a hint of lavender. They appear in April, in clusters of bells that hang suspended above the plants. The leaves are unusual and attractive—broad, smooth, and a pale blue-green with a

SHADE

SHADE

vague resemblance to tulip foliage. During the growing season, Virginia bluebells thrive in moist shade, but once they go dormant, a place that becomes dry in summer suits them fine.

NATIVE HABITAT AND RANGE: Moist woods from New York, west to Kansas and south to Alabama.

USDA HARDINESS ZONES: 4 to 8

HABIT, USE, AND COMPANIONS: Upright, but relaxed in habit, Virginia bluebells swiftly multiply along running rootstocks and by self-sowing. The mass of spring flowers is wonderfully showy and mixes well with daffodils and early tulips. However, when Virginia bluebells fade, their large leaves turn yellowish-cream, inviting slugs and sprawling over neighbors. One must endure their aftermath for the sake of their beauty; plant Virginia bluebells in spots where, after bloom, they will be camouflaged by emerging perennials and ferns such as lady fern (*Athyrium filix-femina*).

CULTIVARS AND RELATED SPECIES: Tall lungwort (*M. paniculata*) is a succulent plant from 2′ to 3′ tall with puckered, oval, blue green leaves. The ½″ nodding flowers open in late spring and early summer. Found in open woods and around bogs from Hudson Bay, south to Michigan, Minnesota, and Washington. Zones 4 to 7.

Pachysandra procumbens
ALLEGHENY SPURGE

Allegheny spurge is sometimes called "American pachysandra," and there is a faint family resemblance to that ubiquitous Japanese spurge (*P. terminalis*). Both plants are evergreen where winters are warm. However, unlike its Asian counterpart, Allegheny spurge is not a wildly spreading plant. Rather, it creeps outward at a regular but dignified pace, funneling its energies into growing better and more handsome with age. Its blossoms are a delightful bonus. White and fragrant, the dense flower spikes appear in early spring before the new growth. Resembling textured leather, the new leaves emerge a glowing, solid, bright green. Very slowly, through the long summer and fall, they darken. By winter, they have a silvery variegation that contrasts with their deep, dark green.

NATIVE HABITAT AND RANGE: Kentucky south to Louisiana and Florida.

USDA HARDINESS ZONES: 4 to 7

HABIT, USE, AND COMPANIONS: An outstanding and underused groundcover for partial to full shade, Allegheny spurge stands about 1′ tall by about 2′ in circumference. It is a great edger along paths or in front of bulbs, perennials, and ferns that die down in win-

Creeping phlox and its taller relative, blue phlox, carpet the forest floor.

ter. Solomon's seal (*Polygonatum biflorum*) is a great companion to arch over Allegheny spurge.

CULTIVARS AND RELATED SPECIES: 'Forest Green' has uniform, shiny green leaves in summer and is much easier to propagate than the species.

Phlox stolonifera
CREEPING PHLOX

A woodland floor alight with the blooms of phlox, like a fantasy spring scene from a Disney cartoon, seems unreal—too good to be true. Yet when creeping phlox carpets a forest floor with flowers, "fairyland" is the first word that comes to mind.

Creeping phlox is a dark green, mat-forming plant whose round leaves disappear under masses of magenta to pink flowers in April. Where winters are warm enough, creeping phlox is evergreen, spreading wherever it isn't shaded out by dense, overhanging plants or heavy leaf litter.

NATIVE HABITAT AND RANGE: Rich woodlands from Pennsylvania to Georgia.

USDA HARDINESS ZONES: 3 to 8

HABIT, USE, AND COMPANIONS: In

SHADE

Although Jacob's ladder looks delicate and fragile, it is a true survivor.

bloom, creeping phlox stands about 6″ tall. Afterward, its dark green leaves reach barely 2″ above the ground. It is a fine finishing plant to soften edges or creep around stones. Its foamy blooms are a great foil for upright, angular companions such as purple toadshade or Solomon's seal.

CULTIVARS AND RELATED SPECIES: Cultivars include 'Bruce's White' and 'Blue Ridge.' The flowers of blue phlox (*P. divaricata*) are more fragrant than creeping phlox and, at 12″, the plant is taller. It has narrow, pointed leaves that are not evergreen and makes a good groundcover in wooded areas, where it can flow over competition. Found in rich woodlands from Quebec to Michigan and south to Georgia and Alabama. Zones 3 to 9.

Polemonium reptans
JACOB'S LADDER
In early spring when Jacob's ladder's foliage first appears, it has a neat, dark green compactness. As the season progresses, its lax stems elongate and, together with its fine, ferny foliage, lend the plant a delicate—almost help-

less—appearance. Jacob's ladder only looks fragile. It is a true survivor. It is not bothered by insects, needs no winter protection, and returns each spring, refreshed and more vigorous. Under the ground, a robust rootstock sends up a steady supply of new green foliage.

After Jacob's ladder bears loose groups of dainty, blue bell-shaped flowers in late April, the whole plant seems to let down. The long, relaxed stalks drape themselves over the ground as they begin to form round seed capsules.

NATIVE HABITAT AND RANGE: Open woods and thickets from New York to Kansas, south to Alabama.

USDA HARDINESS ZONES: 3 to 8

HABIT, USE, AND COMPANIONS: Jacob's ladder's long stalks don't stand up to their 20″, but sprawl loosely, which makes the plant difficult to place and use. Because it prefers a nearly neutral pH of 6 to 7, growing it among rocks or at the edge of a stone or concrete path is a good idea. A little nip, here and there, with the pruning shears will keep it neat. Too thin by itself to function as groundcover, the key to using it for this purpose is a good companion. Those with contrasting and uniform foliage, such as wild ginger or wild stonecrop (*Sedum ternatum*),

would work well, as would low sedges such as bright apple-green sedge (*Carex austrocaroliniana*).

CULTIVARS AND RELATED SPECIES: 'Blue Pearl' bears a profusion of rich medium blue flowers. 'Lambrook Manor' has showy, outward-facing, lilac blue flowers on 2′-tall plants.

Sanguinaria canadensis
BLOODROOT

Bloodroot's great charm is a ritual of bloom that begins in March with the emergence of the first tightly rolled leaf, protectively curled around a flower bud. Only when it reaches a safe height does the round, lobed leaf unfurl and release a pure white flower around a yellow stamens. Bloodroot's flowers can be exceedingly short-lived. An unseasonably hot day will hasten them to maturity so that a stray breeze shatters them. The transience of blossoms adds poignance to the ritual.

The names derive from bloodroot's red sap. Once used for war paint, the sap stains.

NATIVE HABITAT AND RANGE: Eastern North America.

USDA HARDINESS ZONES: 3 to 8

HABIT, USE, AND COMPANIONS: Growing only about 10″ tall, but spreading broadly along its rootstalk and by seeds that are carried by ants, bloodroot is best

SHADE

seen close up along a path or in the front of a woodland border.

In the wild, bloodroot grows in colonies, covering lightly wooded, moderately moist slopes. This and bloodroot's tendency to self-sow in the sand between paving stones suggest that it needs good drainage. Dutchman's breeches (*Dicentra cucullaria*), with its frothy, gray-green leaves, and delicate bladder fern (*Cystopteris fragilis*) are good companions that enjoy the same pH of 6 to 7.

CULTIVARS AND RELATED SPECIES: 'Multiplex' produces many-petaled, double white flowers that last longer than the species'.

Stylophorum diphyllum
WOOD POPPY
Wood poppy, also often called celandine poppy, lights up shady gardens with a host of cheerful

Wood poppy

golden buttercup flowers. Enormously adaptable, wood poppy can grow and bloom anywhere. The gardener should place wood poppies thoughtfully in the least auspicious sites of the garden and watch them carefully. Their astonishing vigor is a godsend only in places where little else will grow.

Its ornately cut, matte green foliage grows dense and quickly becomes a seamless blanket—a luxuriance in low light conditions.

NATIVE HABITAT AND RANGE: Eastern U.S.

USDA HARDINESS ZONES: 4 to 8

HABIT, USE, AND COMPANIONS: Because of its robust nature and ability to reproduce, wood poppy is best used in places too challenging for other plants to thrive and bloom. The vase-shaped plants grow to 20″ and shade out lower-growing neighbors, a useful characteristic in establishing a garden in a weedy area, but a hazard for shorter, desirable plants. Young wood poppies are easy to pull up; old ones are not. A watchful eye and a lightning-quick trowel will keep wood poppy in place and away from less robust treasures. Virginia bluebell is one companion that can stand up to wood poppy, if only because Virginia bluebell goes dormant at just about time wood poppy matures.

CULTIVARS AND RELATED SPECIES: None available.

Tellima grandiflora
FRINGECUPS

A native of the Pacific Northwest, fringecups will easily naturalize in partial to full shade as long as it has moist soil. When well sited, it is utterly carefree. At first glance, it's possible to mistake fringecups for foamflowers (*Tiarella* species), a Saxifrage relative. Like those of foamflowers, fringecups' leaves grow from a central rosette. They are larger and more hairy—on both the rippled upper and lower surfaces—than most foamflowers. A heart-shaped outline, cut into rounded lobes on the outside margin of each leaf, gives it a lacy valentine look. Fringecups' leaves are a mottled yellow and green with dark veins that suggest stained glass. In May, yellowish flowers, shaped like tiny fringed cups, bloom along tall, 18″ stalks.

NATIVE HABITAT AND RANGE: Low woodlands of the Pacific Northwest.

USDA HARDINESS ZONES: 4 to 9

HABIT, USE, AND COMPANIONS: Fringecups stands about 6″ high, but radiates out a foot from its central rosette. When happily situated, it produces new plants by runners and by seed. It is adaptable, accommodating, generally pest-free, and, thanks to its hirsutism, seems to be slug-proof. A few plants are a pleasant accent

Cultivars of fringecups are available with red flowers, although the species has yellow flowers.

along a woodland path. As a groundcover, fringecups won't spread evenly. The cunning gardener can fill the spaces it leaves uncovered with ferns and trilliums. As an edging, its rounded leaves give it a formal look. Its understated yellow variegation makes it a good companion to the mountain male fern (*Dryopteris oreades*), yellow *Acorus* species, and variegated hostas.

CULTIVARS AND RELATED SPECIES: 'Perky' has smaller leaves than the species and red flowers.

SHADE

Foamflower

Tiarella cordifolia
FOAMFLOWER

The frothy drifts of white that grace woodlands in the spring are courtesy of the plant whose common name is particularly apt: foamflower. On each plant, flower stalks held above the leaves are composed of dozens of tiny white blossoms. One rarely sees a single foamflower. This plant rambles through woodland along far-reaching stolons (stems that run along the ground, forming new plants) to create large, freeform drifts. Foamflower's leaves—generally lobed, variegated, and heart-shaped—are as lovely as its flowers.

NATIVE HABITAT AND RANGE: Moist woods from Nova Scotia and Ontario south to Georgia and west to Indiana, Michigan, and Minnesota.

USDA HARDINESS ZONES: 4 to 8

HABIT, USE, AND COMPANIONS: Foamflower's leaves radiate out from a central rosette that stands about 6″ tall or about 1′ tall when the plant is in flower in April or May. A classic woodland ground-cover, foamflower thrives in a moist and moderately acid to neutral soil and blooms in fairly dense shade. It is pretty with false Solomon's seal (*Smilacina racemosa*) and clumpers like the Christmas fern (*Polystichum acrostichoides*).

CULTIVARS AND RELATED SPECIES: In recent years, the variability of the leaves has inspired nurserymen to produce a bewildering array of cultivars and selections. 'Eco Running Tapestry', 'Filigree Lace', and 'Oakleaf' are some of these, and their names say it all. Some of the foamflowers now available commercially include non-running types that stay put.

Trillium cuneatum
PURPLE TOADSHADE

In addition to "purple toadshade," this wildflower has been called "whippoorwill flower," "bloody butcher," and "sweet Betsy." The host of common names with conflicting connotations is not surprising. This is a trillium to be reckoned with—an early spring-blooming, big, bold trillium of darkly organic coloring.

It is the largest sessile (meaning the flower, having no "neck," sits directly upon the leaves) trillium in the East, standing up to 20″ tall. Three substantial leaves, often marbled gray, spread out stiffly, framing the flower. The long-lasting flowers hold their three petals upright. The petals are often maroon, but may be yellow, chartreuse, or bronze. Some smell good, like a faint whiff of sweet shrub (*Calycanthus* species), while others have an unpleasant odor.

One of the easiest trilliums to grow, purple toadshade doesn't take long to form a large colony. When it does, the effect is spectacular. In the wild, purple toadshade grows most magnificently on limestone or shale bluffs and favors sloping sites.

NATIVE HABITAT AND RANGE: Rich, upland woods of Southern Kentucky, Tennessee west of the Appalachians; North Carolina, east of the mountains, and south to Mississippi and Alabama.

USDA HARDINESS ZONES: 5 to 8

HABIT, USE, AND COMPANIONS: Purple toadshade can hold its own

A yellow form of purple toadshade

a little back from a path or from the front of a woodland border. Its height allows it to share a space with lower growing plants such as wood phlox, wild gingers, or Allegheny spurge.

CULTIVARS AND RELATED SPECIES: Prairie trillium (*T. recurvatum*) is also sessile but has smaller leaves and red-brown flowers. Yellow trillium (*T. luteum*) has chartreuse to lemon yellow flowers and smells of lemons.

Trillium grandiflorum
GREAT WHITE TRILLIUM

Trilliums have always seemed to possess a magical aura. In the past they were deemed too untamed for the cultivated garden. While it is indeed an amazing flower to come upon in the wilderness, the great white trillium is

Despite its wild origins, great white trillium is carefree in the garden.

turning from white to rosy pink as they mature. The leaves are a clean, unmottled green. As the plant ages, it tends to clump rather than spread singly as do some other trilliums, making it more striking with each passing year.

NATIVE HABITAT AND RANGE: Open woods and slopes from Quebec to Ontario and south to North Carolina, Missouri, and Minnesota.

USDA HARDINESS ZONES: 3 to 8

HABIT, USE, AND COMPANIONS: Older plants that have spread wider than their height of about 18″ look like low-growing shrubs. This shrubby habit is especially pleasing when the plant is grown among rocks. The dwarf lady fern (*Athyrium filix-femina* 'Minutissimum'), growing a feathery 12″ tall, is a splendid companion. Later on, when the great white trillium dies down in summer, its vacated space may be filled with the fall blooming white wood aster (*Aster divaricatus*).

CULTIVARS AND RELATED SPECIES: Snow trillium (*T. nivale*) is a small plant with egg-shaped, gray green leaves and tiny snow-white flowers in earliest spring. Found in rich, rocky deciduous woods, on outcroppings, and river bluffs from Pennsylvania and Minnesota, south to West Virginia and Nebraska. Zones 4 to 8.

also a fine, hardy, carefree garden plant. If there is any mystery surrounding it, it is that of origin. Because it takes about 7 years from seed to flower, many of the trilliums sold have been dug out of our national parklands. Taking care to buy trilliums that have been nursery propagated from reliable sources will ensure that you have acquired a healthy plant without contributing to the depletion of trilliums in the wild.

An excellent plant for the woodland garden, the great white trillium blooms for a full month—usually late April into May, its flowers

Uvularia grandiflora
GREAT MERRYBELLS

After a year or two in the ground, great merrybells begin to form fine colonies that are a welcome sight in the spring garden. Their foliage is arresting: elegantly arching, forking stalks are clasped by long, cascading green leaves. Among the leaves are dangling bell flowers, echoing the long shape of the leaves. They are also often called "large-flowered bellwort."

Each bloom is a lovely corn-yellow with a hint of green, only a few shades removed from the pale green of the foliage. In the generally subdued world of woodland plants, great merrybells are more quietly elegant than most, yet they never fail to draw attention. They disappear in summer.

NATIVE HABITAT AND RANGE: Moist slopes in woodlands from Quebec to Ontario and south to Georgia, Kansas, and Minnesota.

USDA HARDINESS ZONES: 3 to 8

HABIT, USE, AND COMPANIONS: A well-grown colony of great merrybells reaches 2′ tall and at least as wide as it spreads by rhizomes through moist, humus-rich soil. Its pale color and strongly cascading habit contrast with just about all of its neighbors and make it an intriguing focus. It is spectacular in combination with maidenhair

Great merrybells

fern and Canada wild ginger (*Asarum canadense*), with its dark, leathery, orbicular leaves. Allegheny spurge is a good groundcover nearby.

CULTIVARS AND RELATED SPECIES: Wild oats (*U. sessilifolia*) is a delicate, running plant with sessile, oval leaves and nodding, straw-colored flowers. Plants weave in and out among ferns and other wildflowers in the spring garden. 'Variegata' has showy leaves with creamy white margins. Found in acidic woods from New England, west to North Dakota, and south in the mountains to South Carolina and Arkansas. Zones 3 to 8.

SHADE

PARTIAL SHADE

WILDFLOWERS FOR PARTIAL SHADE

by Kim Hawks

Hubrecht's bluestar

Amsonia hubrectii
HUBRECHT'S BLUESTAR

I'm in love with this particular bluestar. It has everything going for it: wonderful, needle-like foliage; numerous, star-shaped, steel-blue flowers in early spring; and the foliage turns banana-yellow in the fall before going dormant. I expect fall color from many of our native trees and shrubs in the fall, but from a perennial? That is indeed more rare than common.

This tough native handles dry or well-drained, partial-shade conditions with ease. It basks in bright or all-morning sunlight. Although it has a restricted native habitat, it is very adaptable in the cultivated garden.

NATIVE HABITAT AND RANGE: Along creeks and stream banks in west-central Arkansas and Oklahoma.

USDA HARDINESS ZONES: 4 to 9

HABIT, USE, AND COMPANIONS: Over time Hubrecht's bluestar makes a striking statement with a soft, rounded form, topping out at 3′ to 4′ with an equal spread. At the Chanticleer gardens in Pennsylvania they are planted *en masse* in a circular parking lot island. I saw them one week before the peak fall color, and they were stunning. The fine texture contrasts nicely with the bold foliage of hostas (especially 'Love Pat', with its blue cupped leaves) or American alumroot (*Heuchera americana*), particularly 'Pewter Veil'.

CULTIVARS AND RELATED SPECIES: The flowers of willow bluestar (*A. tabernaemontana*) are, like Hubrecht's, star-shaped and steel-blue. However, the leaves of willow bluestar are lance-shaped like weeping willow's. It has a loose, round form of 3′ to 4′.

Aquilegia canadensis
EASTERN WILD COLUMBINE

Upward-pointing, deep coral-red spurs with lemon-yellow petals appear in early spring. Deep within these bell-shaped, tubular flowers, nectar waits to be sipped by early migrating hummingbirds. The flowers emerge from 3′ stalks atop a loose mound of compound, 3-lobed leaflets.

Eastern wild columbine detests poorly drained areas but will give years of beauty in open shade, where it may naturalize by seeding in. If this is not desired, simply remove the flowering stalks just below the foliage as soon as the flowers fade.

NATIVE HABITAT AND RANGE: Rocky, wooded, or open slopes from Ontario to Quebec; south through New England to Florida and Texas; west to Tennessee and Wisconsin.

USDA HARDINESS ZONES : 2 to 8

HABIT, USE, AND COMPANIONS: This is one of the few native plants with bright coral-red flowers. It contrasts well with the floating blue flowers of blue phlox (*P. divaricata*), or echoes the butter-yellow blossoms of celandine poppy (*Stylophorum diphyllum*).

CULTIVARS AND RELATED SPECIES: 'Corbett' is shorter than the species, with soft primrose-yellow

Eastern wild columbine

flowers. Western wild columbine (*A. formosa*) is the western U.S. version of eastern wild columbine, with similar flowers of bright yellow and red spurs atop 3′ plants. Flowering occurs in late spring through early summer.

Aruncus dioicus
GOATSBEARD

Sprays of graceful, pure white flower plumes command attention in early summer. This is a bold plant when in bloom, as a 6′ leafstalk of compound leaflets pushes forth plumes of frothy flowers.

Bright, diffused light and

Goatsbeard

moist, rich soil keeps goatsbeard in heavy bloom. In deep shade, blooms are sparse, but this wildflower tolerates full sun if sited in a consistently moist soil.

NATIVE HABITAT AND RANGE: Pennsylvania south to Georgia, west to Alabama, Kentucky, Arkansas, and Pacific Northwest.

USDA HARDINESS ZONES: 3 to 8

HABIT, USE, AND COMPANIONS: Plant goatsbeard as a backdrop to woodland ferns, native alumroot, wild bleeding heart (*Dicentra eximia*), and hostas, or let it pop up through low groundcovers such as green and gold (*Chrysogonum virginianum*), carpet

bugleweed (*Ajuga reptans*), or perennial geranium species. Plants are either male or female, but because the male flowers are showier, most nurseries offer only male plants. A male or female plant is worth having in the garden for early summer color.

CULTIVARS AND RELATED SPECIES: None widely available.

Aster divaricatus
WHITE WOOD ASTER

This quietly charming aster is happy in the shade and blooms from late summer through early fall in the partial-shade garden. It is easy to grow; select a spot in diffused light with moisture-retentive soil that is enriched with organic matter. White wood aster is tolerant of dry summertime spells. The small but numerous flowers have single petals with yellow centers that brighten up shade gardens. Black, twiggy stems provide a showy contrast to white flowers. As the season passes, the flowers turn a subtle burgundy and rose-pink.

NATIVE HABITAT AND RANGE: Dry, open woods from New England to Ohio, south to Georgia and Alabama.

USDA HARDINESS ZONES: 3 to 8

HABIT, USE, AND COMPANIONS: Whether planted in masses or placed here and there as high-

PARTIAL SHADE

lights, white wood aster is a must in the shade garden. It carpets the earth with flowers like snowflakes. It has a casual, loose, sprawling habit, forming a 1' to 2' groundcover of arrow-shaped, serrated leaves. White wood aster looks great just behind American alumroot or near the purple-spotted, late-summer flowers of toad lily (*Tricyrtis* species). Or, plant white wood aster as a carpet beneath woodland trees, such as sweet bay magnolia (*M. virginiana*) or eastern redbud (*Cercis canadensis*).

CULTIVARS AND RELATED SPECIES: *Aster cordifolius* is a bit larger, to 3', with heart-shaped leaves and sky-blue to white flowers. 'Little Caro' has mounds of sky-blue flowers on 2' plants. Native to open woods from Nova Scotia and Georgia, west to Minnesota and Missouri. Zones 4 to 8.

Caltha palustris
MARSH MARIGOLD
Shiny, butter-yellow flowers cluster among wavy, heart-shaped leaves rising from thick, hollow, branching stems. Marsh marigold is a short wetland plant of 5" to 7" whose flowers resemble buttercups rather than marigolds. It adds

Marsh marigold brings bright splashes of color to wetlands or bog areas.

Pink turtlehead

grassy clumps of white-bracted sedge (*Rhynchospora latifolia*), with its showy, pure white flowers dipped in green.

CULTIVARS AND RELATED SPECIES: 'Alba' is a robust cultivar with white flowers that bloom for 3 to 4 weeks. 'Flore Pleno', also sold as 'Multiplex', is a fast-growing selection with double flowers.

Chelone lyonii
PINK TURTLEHEAD

Pink turtlehead is a late summer-blooming native for light shade. The distinctive, reddish purple flowers nestle atop colonies of 3'- to 4'-tall stems. The flower's shape and a spot of purple make it resemble a turtle's head. Pink turtlehead is versatile, tolerating well-drained sites as well as poorly drained areas. The wetter the site, the more sun it can take.

NATIVE HABITAT AND RANGE: Moist areas in clearings or diffused light in the southern Appalachian Mountains of North Carolina, South Carolina, Georgia, and Tennessee.

USDA HARDINESS ZONES: 3 to 8

HABIT, USE, AND COMPANIONS: Although it tolerates dry soils, pink turtlehead is happiest in moist, poorly drained areas. In well-drained areas, pink turtlehead pops up through 'Burgundy Glow' carpet bugleweed or coex-

springtime color to boggy areas that get bright or diffused sun, then goes dormant in summer.

NATIVE HABITAT AND RANGE: Swamps, marshes, wet meadows, pond edges, and stream banks in boreal areas of North America, south to North Carolina, west to Iowa and Nebraska and into Alaska.

USDA HARDINESS ZONES: 2 to 8

HABIT, USE, AND COMPANIONS: Marsh marigold dapples soggy landscapes with tight clumps of sunshine-yellow. For stunning wetland compositions, add some pickerel weed (*Pontederia cordata*) to provide a contrast of vertical 1' spikes of blue, or the

ists easily with deadnettles (*Lamium maculatum* 'Beedham's White' or 'Beacon Silver'). In poorly drained areas, plant with woodland ferns, blue flag iris (*I. versicolor*), or great blue lobelia (*L. siphilitica*).

CULTIVARS AND RELATED SPECIES: Smooth turtlehead (*C. glabra*) has lance-shaped leaves and white flowers tinted with purple. Plants form open clumps with 2' to 4' stalks. Found in wetlands and low meadows from Newfoundland and Georgia, west to Minnesota and Alabama. Zones 3 to 8.

Black cohosh

Cimicifuga racemosa
BLACK COHOSH, BUGBANE

This audacious wildflower commands attention as its pure white flowering spikes reach 6' to 8', creating a candelabrum of light in shady areas. The odor of this plant is believed to repel bugs (hence the common name "bugbane")—all the more reason to grow it.

Black cohosh thrives in moist, humusy, rich soil, though is is a bit slow to become established and fill out; the patient gardener will be rewarded with its beauty. Plant it where it will not be touched by harsh afternoon sun. Despite its tall stature, it does not require staking.

NATIVE HABITAT AND RANGE: Rich woods and clearings from Southern Ontario, Massachusetts, south to Georgia, and west to Tennessee and Missouri.

USDA HARDINESS ZONES: 3 to 8

HABIT, USE, AND COMPANIONS: Large, compound, sharply serrated leaves bear vertical, leafy stalks of white flowers in early summer. The white, spiked blossoms can accent the white and pink-tinged fronds of Japanese painted ferns (*Athyrium niponicum* var. *pictum*), or the contrasting foliage of hostas, especially plants with white variegation. Great blue lobelia echoes black

Umbrella plant

cohosh's tall spikes.

CULTIVARS AND RELATED SPECIES:
The southeastern U.S. species
Kearney's bugbane (*C. rubifolia*)
complements cool, moist woodland gardens with its slender,
wand-like racemes of white.

Darmera peltata
UMBRELLA PLANT
In early spring, large glistening
leaves pop open like umbrellas
behind clusters of starry pink
flowers. Although the 2'-tall flowers are not showy, the plants give
a lush, tropical look to wet areas.

Though it grows in shady

bogs, the wetter the site, the more
sun it tolerates. Umbrella plant is
also at home in dense, wet clay,
where few plants volunteer to live.
NATIVE HABITAT AND RANGE:
Mountain streams from southern
Oregon to northern Canada.
USDA HARDINESS ZONES: 4 to 8
HABIT, USE, AND COMPANIONS:
Anchor corners of water gardens
with a showy mound of umbrella
foliage, or plant where the low
angle of light at sunrise and sunset can filter through the 18" to
24" leaves. Give it plenty of room,
whether it is alone or in the company of other robust, moisture-
loving plants, such as southern
blue flag iris (*I. virginica*).
CULTIVARS AND RELATED SPECIES:
None available.

Dicentra eximia
WILD BLEEDING HEART
Delicate, fern-like foliage, subtly
tinted blue-green, and tiny, nodding pink flowers throughout
spring and sporadically during the
summer make this an indispensable plant for the woodland garden. Grow in humus-rich, moist,
yet well-drained soil; avoid soggy
areas. Bright, diffused light is best.
NATIVE HABITAT AND RANGE:
Open woods from New York,
south to Georgia, west to Tennessee and West Virginia.
USDA HARDINESS ZONES: 3 to 9

HABIT, USE, AND COMPANIONS:
Softly rounded mounds, 18" high, of feathery foliage nestle comfortably near the front of the border. Clustered, heart-shaped flowers open along stems that pop up through the foliage and gently arch over. Wild bleeding heart constrasts well with the fans of dwarf crested iris (*I. cristata*), the smooth, heart-shaped leaves of wild ginger, the subtle white mottling of Allegheny spurge (*Pachysandra procumbens*), or the delicate spikes of foamflower (*Tiarella cordifolia*).
CULTIVARS AND RELATED SPECIES:
Western bleeding heart (*D. formosa*) is similar to its eastern cousin in leaf and flower, though the blossoms are larger and it has a spreading rather than clumping habit. Although it is native to the western U.S., I have grown it successfully in my southeastern garden in a bright, northern exposure.

Wild bleeding heart

many other woodland treasures.

American alumroot grows effortlessly in woodsy soil enriched with leaf mold or compost, in diffused or bright light. Pick a spot with afternoon shade and you'll be rewarded with colorful foliage summer through frost.
NATIVE HABITAT AND RANGE:
In woods, shady slopes, and rocky outcroppings from Ontario, New England, and Michigan, south to Georgia, west to Alabama, and into Oklahoma.
USDA HARDINESS ZONES: 4 to 9
HABIT, USE, AND COMPANIONS:
Olive-green or burgundy, almost leafless stems push up 2' flowering stalks of tiered, tiny, apple-

Heuchera americana
AMERICAN ALUMROOT
This plant has lovely, tiny, green flowers, but its beautiful foliage is its strongest trait. American alumroot's leaves are green and burgundy with shiny silver sheen or highlights. Scalloped, heart-shaped leaves form full 1' to 2' mounds that coexist happily with

PARTIAL SHADE

Southern blue flag iris is a bold, tall wildflower that likes to have wet feet.

green buds that become greenish flowers. Pleasing combinations are endless. To play off the burgundy colors in late summer, plant American alumroot in front of carpet bugleweed (*Ajuga reptans* 'Burgundy Glow'), a variegated pink groundcover; the white and pink fronds of Japanese painted fern; or pink turtlehead. Laurentia (*Laurentia fluviatilis*) with tight, ground-hugging foliage and soft, powder blue flowers could weave around the base of American alumroot. Great blue lobelia's summertime spikes bring out the subtle blue in American alumroot's foliage. Two native sedge species, *Carex eburnea* and *C. pen-* *sylvanica*, offer contrasting, grassy foliage to nestle near American alumroot.

CULTIVARS AND RELATED SPECIES: Thanks to the breeding work of Dan Heims and several other noted growers, there are numerous cultivars available to today's gardeners; most offer slightly different variegations, though work is being done to produce showier flowers. Hairy alumroot (*H. villosa*) is another fabulous southeastern native with hairy stems and round, lobed leaves, complete with showy panicles of creamy white flowers in late summer. En masse, it is a show-stopper and further extends the alumroot season.

Iris virginica
SOUTHERN BLUE FLAG IRIS

Hard to find in the trade, this is a knock-out iris with strong, fat, vertical fans that arch over at the tips and bear early summer flowers of violet-blue splotched with yellow. Native to wetlands, find a poorly drained or frequently damp spot (everybody has a ditch!) and you'll be rewarded with its beauty and ease of growth.

NATIVE HABITAT AND RANGE: Wetlands from Virginia to Florida and Texas.

USDA HARDINESS ZONES: 7 to 8

HABIT, USE, AND COMPANIONS: This is a vigorous iris with bold, dense, 4′ foliage that provides a strong vertical accent in the partial-shade to full-sun garden. Find a wet site, perhaps next to a pond, near pickerel weed, or in front of the pure white, early summer spires of Virginia sweetspire (*Itea virginica*). Southern blue flag iris also thrives in moist yet well-drained sites with a myriad of pleasing companions, including prairie phlox (*Phlox pilosa*), sundrop (*Oenothera fruticosa*), or showy primrose (*Oenothera speciosa*). It looks great popping through the sunshine-yellow foliage of the groundcover, golden creeping jenny (*Lysimachia nummularia* 'Aurea').

CULTIVARS AND RELATED SPECIES: Blue flag iris (*I. versicolor*) is similar, although its sword-like foliage tops out at 2′ to 3′, and it has slightly smaller flowers and a yellow-based sepal. Its culture is the same as southern blue flag iris.

Lobelia cardinalis
CARDINAL FLOWER

In Chapel Hill, North Carolina, Labor Day is ushered in with the 3′ to 4′ spikes of blood-red cardinal flower. Hummingbirds love cardinal flower, and it thrives in a moist, lightly shaded area, such as along a stream. In autumn,

Cardinal flower

remove any fallen tree leaves, as the rosettes need the winter sun to survive. Allow the plants to go to seed and, eventually, you'll be rewarded with a dense colony of brilliant red in late summer.

NATIVE HABITAT AND RANGE: Low meadows and alongside creeks from southern Ontario and Quebec to New Brunswick and Minnesota, south to Florida, and west to eastern Texas.

USDA HARDINESS ZONES: 2 to 9

HABIT, USE, AND COMPANIONS: From flat rosettes rise multiple flowering spikes that bear numerous tubular, bright red flowers. Small, 5-petaled flowers are intri-

cate, comprising 2 upper lips and 3 lower lips. Plant at the back of a wet area with native ferns in the foreground and some Virginia spiderwort (*Tradescantia virginica*) nearby. The flowers of white turtlehead (*Chelone glabra*) contrast nicely with the intense red of cardinal flower.

CULTIVARS AND RELATED SPECIES: While the tubular flower is similar to cardinal flower's, great blue lobelia (*L. siphilitica*) bears shorter multiple spikes of 2' to 3' blue flowers in late summer. It also tolerates a dryer site and more sun than cardinal flower, residing happily in a lightly shaded garden with moist yet well-drained soil.

Western skunk cabbage

Lysichiton americanum
WESTERN SKUNK CABBAGE

Dramatic, late-winter flowers and bold foliage make this an eye-catching native for soggy woodland areas. Skunk cabbage thrives where most other plants fail, in partially shady spots with poor drainage. Its common name comes from the musky odor of both the flowers and foliage, but it is not overly offensive and should not deter gardeners from growing this great wetland native.

NATIVE HABITAT AND RANGE: Wetlands, swamps, and wet woodlands in western North America.

USDA HARDINESS ZONES: 7 to 9
HABIT, USE, AND COMPANIONS:
Gardeners are rewarded with a jump on spring when soft yellow, open ovate sheaves surrounding a vertical green flower appear in late winter. The curious yet showy flowers bloom without foliage and, although the 2′ flowers hover near the ground, they are quite noticeable, as the rest of the woodland is still dormant and not visible. After flowering, lush, glossy leaves claim their space, choking out even the most persistent weeds. Plant cardinal flower close by to provide color at the end of the season. Ferns provide a pleasing contrast.
CULTIVARS AND RELATED SPECIES: None available.

Phlox divaricata × laphamii × pilosa 'Chattahoochee'
CHATTAHOOCHEE PHLOX
This native groundcover, with periwinkle-blue, 5-petaled flowers and an enchanting maroon eye, is at home in many places in the springtime garden. Although Chattahoochee phlox seems to detest growing in a pot and looks insignificant at the nursery, it fills out nicely if you plant it in a spot that receives half a day of direct sun to bright filtered sunlight. After flowering, cut back to help it tighten up.

NATIVE HABITAT AND RANGE: The species that are crossed in this hybrid occur throughout the U.S.
USDA HARDINESS ZONES: 4 to 8
HABIT, USE, AND COMPANIONS:
This sprawling phlox provides a pleasing carpet under the pinkish purple, tulip-shaped flowers of saucer magnolia (*Magnolia soulangeana*)—the maroon eye matches the magnolias. Intermingle with blue muscari or carpet bugleweed 'Jungle Beauty', or plant beneath the delicate blossoms of pink loropetalum (*L. chinensis* var. *rubra*).

Chattahoochee phlox

PARTIAL SHADE

Wild sweet William, available in many colors such as 'Alpha', is an excellent wildflower for smaller gardens, as it never grows very tall.

CULTIVARS AND RELATED SPECIES:
Wild blue phlox (*P. divaricata*) is a parent of 'Chattahoochee', with soft, sky-blue flowers and a heavenly scent. The oval, evergreen leaves form an open groundcover. Plants reseed freely and create lovely drifts. There are many named selections in a range of colors, including white. Found in open woods and flood plains from Quebec and Georgia, west to Minnesota and Texas. Zones 3 to 9.

Phlox maculata
WILD SWEET WILLIAM
Considered a mainstay for herbaceous borders in partial shade or full sun, this 2′ to 3′ phlox provides rounded heads of mauve-pink flowers in early summer. Because of its short stature, it is an excellent choice for smaller gardens. Grow in soil amended with organic matter. Wild sweet William tolerates slightly damp sites as well as well-drained areas.

NATIVE HABITAT AND RANGE:
Moist roadsides in Virginia, Georgia, Tennessee, Kentucky, and West Virginia

USDA HARDINESS ZONES: 3 to 8

HABIT, USE, AND COMPANIONS:
Plant near the front to the middle of the border in full sun or open, diffused light. Wild sweet William goes well with other early sum-

mer-blooming perennials, such as the creamy white flowers of double Japanese aster (*Kalimeris pinnatifida*) or 'Becky's Shasta Daisy' (*Leucanthemum × superbum*). Accent with the burgurndy color and contrasting, feathery foliage of bronze fennel (*Foeniculum vulgare* var. *purpureum*). Grow dwarf or compact daylilies or creeping verbena (*V. canadensis*) at the feet of wild sweet William.

CULTIVARS AND RELATED SPECIES: Numerous cultivars are available, selected for traits such as powdery mildew resistance, and colors such as pure white, to white with a purple eye, to rose-pink.

nials. Bright white to pinkish white flowers perched on mahogany stems lighten up the summer shade garden. Other pleasing companions are the small- to medium-leaved hostas, the heart-shaped leaves of American alumroot, and woodland ferns.

CULTIVARS AND RELATED SPECIES: American ipecac (*P. stipulatus*) is similar but has a more open habit. The leaves are deeply toothed, and the petioles bear persistent stipules that give the plant a winged look. Found in open woods from New York and Georgia, west to Illinois and Texas. Zones 4 to 9.

Porteranthus (formerly *Gillenia*) *trifoliatus*
BOWMAN'S-ROOT
Starry, ethereal flowers on wiry, branched stems add an airy feel to the woodland garden. Bowman's-root thrives in dappled or open sun as long as the harsh afternoon sunlight is avoided. Plant in well-drained, acidic soil.

NATIVE HABITAT AND RANGE: Wooded uplands of northeastern U.S. and Canada.

USDA HARDINESS ZONES: 4 to 8

HABIT, USE, AND COMPANIONS: Equally at home in the herbaceous border or the woodland garden, bowman's-root plays a supporting role to other showy peren-

Smilacina racemosa
FALSE SOLOMON'S SEAL
Burnt orange-red berries with purple spots hang at the ends of arching 2′ to 3′ branches and light up the woodland garden in fall. Grow in dappled shade in soil rich in organic matter with good drainage.

NATIVE HABITAT AND RANGE: Woodland areas from Nova Scotia and British Columbia, south to Georgia, west to Arizona and California.

USDA HARDINESS ZONES: 3 to 8

HABIT, USE, AND COMPANIONS: False Solomon's seal is highly adaptable to a variety of locations in the woodland garden. The satiny foliage bears fluffy, white terminal flower spikes in spring. It combines beautifully with ferns, wild bleeding heart, and Japanese roof iris (*I. tectorum*), In the fall, when the distinctive berries of false Solomon's seal appear in clusters at the end of the stems, the bronzy foliage of autumn fern (*Dryopteris erythrosora*) makes a stellar combination.

CULTIVARS AND RELATED SPECIES: Starry Solomon's plume (*S. stellata*) is a delicate plant with lance-shaped to narrow oval, blue-green leaves and small clusters of starry white flowers. The showy berries are bright green with red stripes. Plants grow in sun or shade in rich soil. Found in woods and on prairies from Newfoundland and Virginia, west to British Columbia and California. Zones 2 to 8.

Solidago flexicaulis
ZIGZAG GOLDENROD

This zigzag-stemmed goldenrod blooms in summer and is easy to grow in open shade or a lightly shaded woodland border.

NATIVE HABITAT: Eastern North America.

USDA HARDINESS ZONES: 4 to 8

HABIT, USE, AND COMPANIONS: Sharply toothed, egg-shaped leaves bear short clusters of flowers in the leaf axils or in a terminal cluster. The zigzagged stem gives a slightly angled appearance on this 2' to 3' goldenrod, complementing the predominantly green textures in the woodland garden. Zigzag goldenrod provides a pleasing canopy over partridge berry (*Mitchella repens*), green and gold, or creeping woodland phlox (*P. stolonifera*). Place some great blue lobelia nearby to offer contrasting blue spikes of 3'.

CULTIVARS AND RELATED SPECIES: Wreath goldenrod (*S. caesia*) has narrow, blue-green leaves mingling along the stem with spikes of yellow flowers. Found in open woods and clearings throughout eastern North America. Zones 4 to 9.

Spigelia marilandica
INDIAN PINK

People are intrigued by the unusual flowers of this woodland plant. Indian pink grows unnoticed until midsummer, when bright, lipstick-red, slightly swollen, trumpet-shaped blossoms open to reveal greenish yellow, 5-petaled, star-like flowers that face skyward. Indian pink prefers dappled shade in well-drained soils with organic matter.

NATIVE HABITAT AND RANGE: Open woodlands from Maryland south to Florida; west to Texas, Missouri, and Oklahoma.

USDA HARDINESS ZONES: 4 to 9

HABIT, USE, AND COMPANIONS:
Because of its small stature of 2′ to 3′, plant Indian pink near a pathway where you can admire the detail of the flowers. Plants with chartreuse foliage that dwell in the shade make stunning combinations: small- to medium-leaved chartreuse hostas or golden club moss (*Selaginella kraussiana* 'Aurea').

CULTIVARS AND RELATED SPECIES:
None available.

Thalictrum thalictroides
RUE ANEMONE
"Drought-tolerant" and "delicate yet tough" are the first descriptions that come to mind for this diminutive, spring-blooming native. The round, lobed leaflets of rue anemone offset its numerous tiny flowers in shades of white, soft pink, or medium pink, which gently float above the foliage.

Bright, diffused light suits this anemone, yielding more flowers and tighter foliage. In summer drought, rue anemone may go dormant, but it faithfully returns the following spring.

NATIVE HABITAT AND RANGE:
In open woods from southwest Maine to northwest Florida; west to Alabama, Mississippi, Arkansas, and Oklahoma; north to Minnesota.

Plant Indian pink near a pathway in dappled sunlight to enjoy its delicate, brightly colored flowers.

USDA HARDINESS ZONES: 3 to 8

HABIT, USE, AND COMPANIONS:
This delicate beauty of 4″ to 8″ deserves front-row placement alongside dwarf crested iris (*Iris cristata*), wild gingers (*Asarum* species), or ground-hugging partridge berry (*Mitchella repens*).

CULTIVARS AND RELATED SPECIES:
'Betty Blake' has apple-green, double flowers and blooms for nearly a month. 'Cameo' is a soft pink double. "Shoaff's Double Pink' is a rich, rosy pink.

PARTIAL SHADE

SUN

WILDFLOWERS FOR SUN

by C. Colston Burrell

Aster novae-angliae
NEW ENGLAND ASTER
The genus *Aster* contains some of the most beautiful and best-known roadside wildflowers and garden perennials. The flowers are so familiar and characteristic that similar flowers in other genera are referred to as "aster-like." New England aster is prized for its mounds of royal purple flowers in late summer.

Plant in evenly moist, humus-rich soil in full sun or light shade. Plants will tolerate wet soil. If soil dries in summer, plants will lose their lower leaves. Plants are prone to flopping without the support of other large perennials and shrubs. To keep them compact, shear them back to 8″ to 12″ in June. Bushy stems will resprout in time to set plenty of buds. Divide clumps every 3 to 4 years in spring or after flowering. New England asters are susceptible to powdery mildew, which turns the leaves dull gray. Keep plants from wilting, which gives the disease a foothold. Dust affected plants with sulfur to control the spread of the disease.

NATIVE HABITAT AND RANGE: Wet meadows, prairies, and pond margins from New England to North Dakota, south to Alabama and New Mexico.
USDA HARDINESS ZONES: 3 to 8
HABIT, USE, AND COMPANIONS: A meadow washed with purple New England asters in September is a memorable sight. Mature plants form dense 3′ to 6′ clumps with stiff, leafy stems crowned by dense clusters of 1″ to 2″ lavender to purple flowers with bright yellow centers. Flower color also varies from pure white to pink and rose. In the garden, combine New England asters with other fall-blooming wildflowers, such as goldenrod, sneezeweed (*Helenium autumnale*), gentians, and turtleheads (*Chelone* species). In borders, the height of most selections relegates them to the rear. Mix with Japanese anemones (*Anemone* × *hybrida*), beautyberry (*Callicarpa* species), and ornamental grasses.
CULTIVARS AND RELATED SPECIES: 'Alma Potschke' has rich, glowing salmon-pink flowers on compact 2′ to 4′ plants. Plants bloom in mid-fall. Another favorite is 'Barr's Pink', with semi-double, bright

SUN

New England aster 'Purple Dome' is a new dwarf cultivar of the classic wildflower that blooms in gardens and along roadsides in late summer.

rose-pink flowers in dense heads on 4′ plants. 'Hella Lacy' has royal purple flowers on tight, 3′ to 4′ clumps. 'Purple Dome' is a new dwarf selection with royal purple flowers on 2′, late-flowering clumps. 'September Ruby' has luscious red flowers on floppy, 3′ to 5′ plants. 'Treasure' has a more open form and lavender-blue flowers on 4′ stems.

Smooth aster (*A. laevis*) is a free-flowering species with lavender-blue flowers in open, elongated clusters on 2′ to 3′ plants. Plants are elegant in formal borders or in drifts in prairie and meadow gardens. This is one of the last asters to bloom in autumn. 'Blue Bird', selected by the Mount Cuba Center in Delaware, is a compact plant with deep sky-blue flowers. Smooth aster is found in meadows, prairies, woodland edges, and roadsides from Maine to British Columbia, south to Georgia and New Mexico. Zones 2 to 7.

Aromatic aster (*A. oblongifolius*), produces wide, low mounds of $1^{1}/_{4}''$ purple flowers in September and October. The fuzzy, oblong foliage and scaly buds create an interesting display

SUN

through the summer season. 'Dream of Beauty', selected by Claude Barr, is shorter in stature and has rose-pink flowers. 'Raydon's Favorite' is a Southern cultivar with mounds of blue-purple flowers in October. Found on dry, sandy to rocky slopes in meadows, prairies, open woods, and roadsides from Pennsylvania to Saskatchewan, south to Alabama and New Mexico. Zone 3 to 8.

Baptisia alba, B. lactea, B. leucantha, and *B. pendula*
WHITE WILD INDIGO
Wild indigos are handsome perennials with colorful spikes of pea-like flowers in blue, yellow, cream, and white. The flowers look like those of lupines, but the habit is quite different. Plants are 2′ to 5′ tall, with three-lobed, sea-green leaves. The inflated, sooty brown seed pods nod in open clusters through the autumn.

Wild indigos thrive on neglect. Plant them in rich, moist but well-drained soils in full sun or light shade. All species are drought-tolerant once established. Wild indigos are slow to establish, as the first year or two they are producing a deep taproot. In time they spread to form huge clumps. Space individual plants at least 3′ apart, as they are difficult to move once the taproot gets established.

NATIVE HABITAT AND RANGE: Open woods, meadows, prairie, and savannas in moist or dry soils from Ontario and Minnesota, south to Florida and Texas.
USDA HARDINESS ZONES: 4 to 8
HABIT, USE, AND COMPANIONS: The tall, white-flowered spikes of wild white indigo are held above dense foliage mounds in late spring and early summer. Use them in meadow and prairie gardens with fire pinks (*Silene virginica*), butterfly weed (*Asclepias tuberosa*), bowman's-root (*Gillenia trifoliata*), and prairie phlox (*Phlox pilosa*). Indigos are dramatic border plants. Use them as exclamation points among rounded forms such as bee balm (*Monarda* species), garden phlox, cranesbills (*Geranium* species), and yarrow (*Achillea* species).
CULTIVARS AND RELATED SPECIES: Creamy wild indigo (*B. bracteata*, formerly *B. leucophaea*) produces compact 1′ to 2′ mounds of foliage with tightly packed, drooping clusters of creamy yellow flowers. The 1″ to 2″ 3-lobed leaves are clothed in soft hairs. Look for this species in early spring before other species bloom. Plant in average, well-drained, sandy or loamy soil in full sun or light shade. Found on sandy prairies, savannas, and in dry, open woods from Michigan and Minnesota, south to Kentucky and Texas. Zones 3 to 9.

Yellow wild indigo (*B. sphaero-carpa*, formerly *B. viridis*) is similar to blue false indigo, but the 6″ to 8″ flower spikes bear bright lemon-yellow flowers. The plants are compact, with leafy stems to 3′. The fabulous, round seed pods are dark gray-brown. Plant in average to rich, moist soil in full sun or light shade. Found in open woods and on roadsides in Arkansas and adjacent states. Zones 4 to 9.

Boltonia asteroides
WHITE BOLTONIA
Boltonia is a late-season perennial with tall mounds of aster-like flowers and lovely foliage. The wild form of this species is seldom seen in cultivation. Most gardeners know this plant only as the selection 'Snowbank'.

Plant boltonia in moist, humus-rich soil in full sun or light shade. In drier soil, plants will be smaller. Plants seldom need staking, but if you wish to keep plants short, cut them back to 10″ to 12″ in early June to encourage compact growth without sacrificing flowers. Overgrown plants should be divided in spring.

NATIVE HABITAT AND RANGE:
Low, open woods, wetland margins, and wet ditches from New Jersey and North Dakota, south to Florida and Texas.

'Snowbank' is a neat, compact white boltonia smothered with bright flowers throughout the fall.

USDA HARDINESS ZONES: 3 to 8
HABIT, USE, AND COMPANIONS: The wealth of ghostly 1″ white daisy-like flowers with bright yellow centers are carried in mounded clusters on 4′ to 6′ stems clothed in gray-green, willow-like foliage that is attractive and neat all summer. Combine boltonias with summer- and fall-blooming plants such as fire weed (*Epilobium angustifolium*), Joe-pye weeds (*Eupatorium* species), and ironweeds (*Vernonia* species). In formal gardens, plant them with smooth aster, turtleheads, and

SUN

Winecups

Japanese anemones. Place them at the back of the border where the full mounds of foliage and flowers will not smother other plants.

CULTIVARS AND RELATED SPECIES: 'Pink Beauty' has a more open form and its pale pink flowers open several weeks before 'Snowbank'. Flower color is brighter where summers are cool. 'Snowbank' is a compact selection to 5', smothered with bright white flowers throughout the fall.

Callirhoe involucrata
WINECUPS, POPPY MALLOW

Winecups are floriferous plants of the Southwest and Great Plains with 5 squared-off petals that together form a 2" flower that resembles a tea cup. Plants have weakly upright to trailing 1' to 3' stems clothed in attractive, deeply dissected leaves. Plants begin blooming in spring and flower for several months on new growth.

Plant in average, well-drained, loamy or sandy soil in full sun or light shade. Established plants have deep taproots that resent disturbance, so set out young plants and do not lift them once they are established.

NATIVE HABITAT AND RANGE: Dry, sandy plains, prairies, and open woods from North Dakota and Montana, south to Missouri and New Mexico; naturalized in the East.

USDA HARDINESS ZONES: 4 to 9

HABIT, USE, AND COMPANIONS: Winecups' sprawling stems make it an excellent weaver, best placed at the front of the border to knit together plantings. The trailing stems creep between or over clumps of plants, and flowers pop up here and there. In rich soils, plants form more dense clumps best used at the edge of a bed or along a path. In prairie gardens, plant them with prairie phlox (*Phlox pilosa*), blanket flower (*Gaillardia* species), and prickly pear (*Opuntia humifusa*). Let the trailing stems spill over a rock wall with sedums, hens and chicks (*Sempervivum* species), and lavender.

CULTIVARS AND RELATED SPECIES:
Standing winecups (*C. digitata*) produces wiry, upright 1′ to 4′ stems and deeply dissected foliage with 5 to 7 narrow, linear lobes that resemble slender fingers. The burgundy-red flowers are borne singly or in open clusters. Some plants have white or light rose flowers. A mature clump in flower is a memorable sight. Plants thrive in well-drained, loamy or sandy soil in full sun or light shade. They tend to flop in the shade, but can be placed to grow up through large perennials or shrubs to support the sprawling stems. Found on dry prairies and in open woods from Missouri and Kansas, south to Texas; naturalized farther east. Zones 4 to 9.

Echinacea pallida
PALE PURPLE CONEFLOWER

Coneflowers are erect perennials with coarse, lance-shaped to oval leaves. The flamboyant, daisy-like flowers have mounded, bristly heads and showy rose or pink petal-like rays held above the foliage. Coneflowers are used medicinally for alleviating skin rashes and stimulating the immune system.

Pale purple coneflower

Plant in average to rich, loamy or sandy soil in full sun or light shade. They grow best with adequate moisture but are quite tolerant of extended drought. Mature plants form stout clumps from deep, fleshy taproots that resent disturbance.

NATIVE HABITAT AND RANGE:
Found in open woods, savannas, and prairies from Illinois to Iowa, south to Arkansas and Oklahoma.

USDA HARDINESS ZONES: 4 to 8

HABIT, USE, AND COMPANIONS:
Pale purple coneflower is a sparsely branching plant with stout, nearly leafless 2′ to 4′ stems topped with large heads of 4″, drooping, pale rose rays. The basal leaves are lance-shaped and clothed in

SUN

stiff hairs. Plant coneflowers in formal gardens with garden phlox (*Phlox paniculata*), blazing stars (*Liatris* species), and globe thistles (*Echinops* species). In meadows and prairies, plant them with butterfly weed, mountain mint (*Pycnanthemum* species), and purple prairie clover (*Dalea purpurea*). The dried seed heads ornament the winter landscape.

CULTIVARS AND RELATED SPECIES: Narrow-leaved coneflower (*E. angustifolia*) is the shortest of the genus, with 1' to 2' stems and spare, lance-shaped basal leaves with stiff hairs. The mostly leafless stems are topped by 2" heads with 1", drooping, rose-pink rays. Plants tolerate alkaline and saline soils. Found on dry prairies and savannas from Saskatchewan and Minnesota, south to Texas. Zones 2 to 8.

Yellow coneflower (*E. paradoxa*) is paradoxical in that its rays are bright yellow. The plants grow 2' to 3' tall in tight, multi-stemmed clumps with mostly basal leaves, which are broadly lance-shaped. Found in open woods and prairies in the Ozark Mountains of Missouri and Arkansas. Zones 4 to 8.

Eupatorium purpureum
SWEET JOE-PYE WEED
Joe-pye weeds are big, bold perennials with opposite or whorled leaves and clouds of small, fuzzy flowers in terminal clusters. The plants form strong multi-stemmed clumps from stout crowns with tough, fibrous roots. The foliage is vanilla-scented when bruised. Joe-pye was a medicine man who believed in the special powers of these plants.

Plant Joe-pye weeds in moist, average to rich soil in full sun or light shade. Established plants need little attention. Young plants reach their full, gargantuan size in 2 years.

NATIVE HABITAT AND RANGE: Seepage slopes, low meadows, woodland edges, and roadsides from New Hampshire to Iowa, south in the mountains to Georgia, and to Oklahoma.

USDA HARDINESS ZONES: 3 to 8

HABIT, USE, AND COMPANIONS: Sweet Joe-pye weed forms beautiful clumps up to 6' tall with billowing crowns of pale rose or light purple, sweet-scented flowers. The 12" leaves are carried in tiered whorls of 4. Joe-pye weeds are equally suited to formal and informal landscapes with bee balms, coneflowers, lilies, sneezeweed, asters, goldenrods (*Solidago* species), and grasses. The skeletonized seed heads are attractive in the winter landscape.

CULTIVARS AND RELATED SPECIES: The 'Atropurpureum' variety is more compact than the wild form, with deep purple stems, dark leaves, and soft raspberry-red, sweetly scented flowers, and may be a hybrid with spotted Joe-pye weed (*E. maculatum*). 'Big Umbrella' is a new German selection with dark stems and huge heads of dark raspberry-red flowers. 'Gateway' is a 6′ giant with mauve flower clusters the size of basketballs.

Spotted Joe-pye weed (*E. maculatum*) is a relatively short species, from 4′ to 6′, with compact, flattened clusters of pale cherry-red to rose-purple flowers. Found in wet prairies, bottomlands, and marshes from Newfoundland and British Columbia, south to Pennsylvania and Oklahoma; also in the mountains to Georgia and New Mexico. Zones 2 to 8.

Gaura lindheimeri
WHITE GAURA
Gaura is an airy plant noted for its long blooming season and heat tolerance. Each flower consists of 4 petals that surround the protruding stamens, which resemble the antennae of a pure white butterfly.

Give gaura average to rich, moist, well-drained soil in full sun. Once established, plants are drought-tolerant. Southern gar-

White gaura tolerates heat well and blooms all summer and into the fall.

SUN

deners prize gaura because it tolerates heat and humidity with aplomb.

NATIVE HABITAT AND RANGE: Open, low woods, prairies, pinelands, and roadsides in Louisiana and Texas.

USDA HARDINESS ZONES: 5 to 9

HABIT, USE, AND COMPANIONS: White gaura is an exuberant, shrubby perennial with upright to lax, 3' to 4' stems carrying spikes of 1" white flowers in a cloud above the 3", deep green foliage. As the flowers age, they blush to pale rose. Gaura blooms all summer and into the autumn. The clumps grow from a thick, deep taproot. Gaura is an excellent see-through plant for borders, meadow gardens, or as a specimen. Combine the airy whirl of flowers with ornamental grasses, blazing stars, butterfly weed, sunflowers, and coneflowers.

CULTIVARS AND RELATED SPECIES: Scarlet gaura (*G. coccinea*) is a daintier plant with 2' stems densely clothed in narrow, 1" leaves. Small rose-pink to red flowers crowd the tips of the stems in spring and early summer. Plant scarlet gaura in average to rich, well-drained soil in full sun. Found on dry prairie ridges, savannas, plains, and roadsides from Indiana and Alberta, south to Missouri, Texas, and California. Zones 3 to 9.

Helianthus angustifolius
SWAMP SUNFLOWER

Sunflowers are robust summer or autumn bloomers with stout, leafy stems from thick, tough rootstock. The brilliant yellow, daisy-like flowers are arrayed in elongated clusters. Individual flowers have prominent, round centers. Birds love the seeds in the ripe heads.

Plant in moist, average to rich soil in full sun. They thrive in wet soil and tolerate drought once established. These large plants require ample room to keep from crowding their neighbors. Plants tend to flop in the wind or when grown in rich soil.

NATIVE HABITAT AND RANGE: Low woods, streambanks, bottomlands, and ditches from New York and Indiana, south to Florida and Texas, mostly along the coastal plain and the lower Mississippi River drainage.

USDA HARDINESS ZONES: 6 to 9; hardy farther north but does not bloom before frost

HABIT, USE, AND COMPANIONS: Swamp sunflower is a masterful plant with stout 4' to 10' stems crowned in September and October with elongated, branching clusters of 3" bright yellow flowers with purple centers. The deep green, lance-shaped leaves are showy in summer. Swamp sunflowers are indispensable additions to the fall garden. Plant them in a meadow or at the back of a large perennial garden. They make a great end-of-season show with the last of the goldenrods, asters, and grasses.

CULTIVARS AND RELATED SPECIES: Willow leaf sunflower (*H. salicifolius*) is a delicate sunflower prized for its narrow, 8″, drooping, gray-green leaves as well as for its flowers. The 2″ flowers are carried in slender, upright clusters throughout the autumn. Plant in average, sandy or loamy, neutral to alkaline, well-drained soil in full sun. Found on dry prairies, savannas, and roadsides from Illinois and Missouri to Kansas and Oklahoma. Zones 4 to 8.

Marsh mallow

SUN

Hibiscus moscheutos
MARSH MALLOW, ROSE MALLOW

Hibiscus are perennials of shrublike structure and proportions. The thick, erect stems are topped by open clusters of huge flowers, each with 5 petals that seem to be made of crepe paper with a long, central bottlebrush that bears the male and female reproductive structures. Their deeply cut, lacy leaves resemble maple's. Individual flowers last only one day, but open in succession for 3 to 6 weeks. The woody seed capsules are quite attractive in fall and winter.

Plant in evenly moist, humus-rich soil in full sun or light shade. Space young transplants at least 3′ apart to allow for their size when mature. Established plants are difficult to transplant and seldom need division. Japanese beetles may skeletonize the leaves. Pick them off and drop them in a pail of soapy water.

NATIVE HABITAT AND RANGE: Wet meadows, low woods, marshes, and ditches from Maryland and Ohio, south to Indiana and Texas.
USDA HARDINESS ZONES: 5 to 10, 4 with protection

HABIT, USE, AND COMPANIONS:
Marsh mallow is a popular perennial with broadly oval leaves with 3 to 5 shallow lobes. The 6" to 8" white flowers with deep red centers are crowded at the upper ends of the stems and open for several months in summer. Plant mallows wherever you need a bold dash of color. They make great specimen plants for a strong accent among shrubs, perennials, and ornamental grasses. Around the margins of a pond, in a pot in a water garden, or in a meadow, plant hibiscus with ferns, iris, astilbes, and ironweed.

CULTIVARS AND RELATED SPECIES:
Marsh mallow (*H. moscheutos* subspecies *palustris*) has 3-lobed leaves and rose-pink or white flowers without an eye. Its native range is confined to coastal areas. Many hybrids have been made combining the compact growth of this species and its color variants with the red flowers of scarlet rose mallow (*H. coccineus.*). The hybrids have huge, 8" to 10" flowers in pure white, white with a crimson eye, pink, rose, and bright red. 'Sweet Caroline' has ruffled, pink flowers with a dark eye. 'Anne Arundel' has 9" pink flowers. 'Lady Baltimore' is pink with a deep red center. 'Lord Baltimore' is deep scarlet.

Scarlet rose mallow (*H. coccineus*) is a stately plant from 5' to 10' tall with broad, deeply incised, palmately lobed or divided leaves, often with red-tinged margins. The 6" saucer-shaped flowers are bright scarlet. Found in wet woods, swamps, and marshes on the coast of Georgia and Florida. Zones 7 to 10.

Seaside mallow (*Kosteletzkya virginica*) is a dainty hibiscus relative with 1' to 4' stalks bearing soft, triangular leaves with a long, pointed, central lobe. The flowers resemble hibiscus, with 3", deep, clear pink flowers carried in clusters at the tops of the stems. Plant in rich, moist to wet soil in full sun. Found in coastal marshes and ditches from New York to Florida and west to Texas. Zones 6 to 9.

Liatris pycnostachya
KANSAS GAYFEATHER, PRAIRIE BLAZING STAR
Liatris are commanding plants with tall spikes bearing dozens of small red-violet to purple flowers gathered in dense spikes or button-like clusters. The spikes open from the top down, an unusual characteristic for a perennial. The grass-like basal leaves are longer and broader than the stem leaves. As the leaves ascend the stem, they reduce in size until they blend into the flowers. Liatris are popular cut flowers.

SUN

Kansas gayfeather makes a striking statement blooming in midsummer.

Plant in rich, evenly moist soil in full sun. Plants are easily overgrown by large, floppy plants, so give them space without competition. The tall stalks may need staking. Mice and voles love to devour the corms.

NATIVE HABITAT AND RANGE: Prairies from Indiana and South Dakota, south to Louisiana and Texas.

USDA HARDINESS ZONES: 3 to 9

HABIT, USE, AND COMPANIONS: Kansas gayfeather is one of the largest and showiest species. The 3′ to 5′ spikes of densely packed, red-violet to mauve flower heads are carried on stiff, leafy stems. The deep green basal leaves are up to 12″ long. Plants bloom in midsummer and are extremely showy when grown in clumps. In meadow and prairie gardens, plant them in the company of other natives, such as golden Alexanders (*Zizia* species), prairie phlox, mountain mints, coneflowers, goldenrods, milkweeds (*Asclepias* species), and ornamental grasses. They add striking vertical form to beds and borders, in contrast to summer blooming perennials such as yarrow and phlox.

CULTIVARS AND RELATED SPECIES: *L. pycnostachya* var. *alba*, also listed as 'Alba', has creamy white flowers but is seed-grown and variable.

Button liatris (*L. ligulistylis*)

SUN

has rounded heads of fuzzy, violet flowers with purple bracts borne in open spikes. Plants grow 2′ to 5′ tall. Plant in humus-rich, evenly moist soil in full sun. Found on wet black-soil prairies and the borders of marshes from Wisconsin and Alberta, south to Colorado and New Mexico. Zones 3 to 8.

Dotted blazing star (*L. punctata*) is a compact, densely clumping plant to 14″ tall with small heads packed tightly into dense, short, 6″ spikes in late summer. The attractive foliage is deep black-green. Plant in well-drained soil in full sun. Found on dry gravel prairies and plains from Manitoba and Alberta, south to Texas and New Mexico. Zones 2 to 8.

Monarda didyma
BEE BALM, OSWEGO TEA

Monardas boast brightly colored, spherical heads of tightly packed, tubular flowers above a circle of colored, leafy bracts. The 1″ flowers have distinctive, protruding upper lips that arch over the smaller, lower ones. Like all mints, the stems are square, the pointed, oval leaves are aromatic, and they grow from fast-creeping runners with fibrous roots. Many garden selections have been named, some of which are hybrids with bergamot (*M. fistulosa*).

Plant in humus-rich, evenly moist soils in full sun or partial shade. If plants dry out, they are more susceptible to powdery mildew. All monardas spread rapidly from creeping stems, and the clumps eventually die out in the center. Divide clumps every 2 to 3 years to keep them vigorous.

NATIVE HABITAT AND RANGE: Moist open woods, shaded roadsides, and clearings from Maine and Michigan, south to New Jersey and Ohio; in the mountains to Georgia.

USDA HARDINESS ZONES: 3 to 8

HABIT, USE, AND COMPANIONS: Bee balm has brilliant flowers in 4″ heads, surrounded by deep red bracts that attract the attention of gardeners and hummingbirds alike. The stout 2′ to 4′ succulent stems form tight clumps. In a moist spot in dappled shade, plant them with queen-of-the-prairie (*Filipendula rubra*), wild sennas (*Cassia* species), turtleheads, ferns, hardy cranesbills, garden phlox, yarrows, and shasta daisies (*Leucanthemum × superbum*).

CULTIVARS AND RELATED SPECIES: 'Blue Stocking' has soft, violet-blue flowers with bright violet bracts. 'Claire Grace' has lavender flowers. 'Jacob Klime' is deep red. 'Marshall's Delight' has clear pink flowers. All of the above cultivars are mildew resistant. 'Prairie Night' has red-violet flowers.

SUN

The brilliant red of bee balm attracts gardeners and hummingbirds alike.

SUN

Foxglove penstemon, also known as beardtongue, is a tall wildflower that originates in wet meadows.

Lemon mint (*Monarda citriodora*) is a charming annual or biennial plant with soft, hairy, 2″, lemon-scented leaves on 2′ stems. The 1½″, deep pink flowers are carried in whorled clusters where the leaves join the stems. They bloom throughout the summer. Plant in average, sandy or loamy soil in full sun or light shade. Found in clearings, woodland edges, and plains from South Carolina and Missouri, south to Florida and Texas. Zones 4 to 9.

Penstemon digitalis
FOXGLOVE PENSTEMON
These wildflowers, also known as beardtongue, are noted for their inflated, irregularly shaped flowers with two upper and three lower lips. Color varies from pink, rose, lavender, and violet to white. The seed capsules are decorative in fall and winter.

Plant in moist, rich soil in full sun or light shade. Plants quickly form dense clumps that need division every 3 to 4 years to keep them healthy. Self-sown seedlings will be numerous.

NATIVE HABITAT AND RANGE:
Wet meadows and prairies, low woods, flood plains, and ditches from Nova Scotia and Minnesota, south to Virginia and Texas.

USDA HARDINESS ZONES: 3 to 8

HABIT, USE, AND COMPANIONS:
Foxglove penstemon is a tall plant to 5′ with open, branched clusters of 1″ white flowers. The 6″ to 8″, toothless, shiny green leaves form tufted rosettes that grow from fibrous roots. In meadows and in soggy spots, combine them with ferns, grasses, bee balm, oxeye (*Heliopsis helianthoides*), and ironweeds. In a formal garden, combine them with cranesbills, ornamental onions, yarrows, Siberian iris, and daylilies.

CULTIVARS AND RELATED SPECIES:
'Husker Red' has deep ruby-red

SUN

The arching branches of the spectacular rough-stemmed goldenrod create a chartreuse haze before the lemon-yellow flowers open in the autumn.

foliage and stems and pink-tinged flowers.

Small's beardtongue (*P. smallii*) is a bushy penstemon with 2′ stems clothed top to bottom in 1″, rose-purple flowers for several weeks in early spring. The glossy, broadly lance-shaped, 4″ leaves have toothed margins. Plants must have good drainage, but are short-lived even under ideal conditions. Give them average; gravely, sandy, or loamy, well-drained soil in full sun or light shade. Found in open woods, woodland margins, and cliffs in the southern Appalachians from North Carolina to Tennessee. Zones 6 to 8.

Solidago rugosa
ROUGH-STEMMED GOLDENROD

Goldenrods flower just as other blooms are slacking off in the garden. The lemon-yellow or golden flowers are carried in plume-like clusters on leafy stems. The silvery seed heads are lovely in early winter.

Plant in average to rich, moist soil in full sun or light shade. Plants spread enthusiastically from creeping rhizomes to form full, gorgeous clumps. Divide plants to control their spread.

NATIVE HABITAT AND RANGE: Found in open woods, meadows,

and old fields from Newfoundland and Michigan, south to Florida and Texas.

USDA HARDINESS ZONES: 4 to 9.
HABIT, USE, AND COMPANIONS: Rough-stemmed goldenrod is a spectacular species with very broad, open flower clusters and arching branches. Plants have leafy stems from 1' to 3½' tall and bloom in October and November. The buds produce an attractive, chartreuse haze before the flowers open. Choose rough-stemmed goldenrod for informal meadows and prairies or formal gardens with asters, sunflowers, phlox, anemones, and grasses. They are beautiful when contrasted with the tropical foliage of bananas, cannas, and elephant ears.
CULTIVARS AND RELATED SPECIES: 'Fireworks' is a superior selection with long chains of flowers in full clusters.

Stiff goldenrod (*S. rigida*) is an unusual species that bears its flowers in large, flattened clusters, creating a showy display of yellow in the late-summer garden. Erect, multi-stemmed clumps rise 2' to 5' from a basal-foliage rosette. The softly hairy, oval foliage is attractive all season and turns dusty rose in autumn. Found on gravel or black-soil prairies, meadows, clearings, and roadsides from Connecticut to Saskatchewan,

south to Georgia and New Mexico. Zones 3 to 9.

S. spathulata is a creeping goldenrod with deep green, paddle-shaped leaves and 1' to 2' inflorescences with stiff, horizontal branches. Plant in average to rich, moist soil in full sun or light shade. 'Golden Fleece' is only 12" tall and is quite floriferous. Found in open, rocky woods, clearings, and on roadsides in limy soils from Virginia and Indiana south to Georgia and Alabama. Zones 4 to 9.

Stokesia laevis
STOKES' ASTER
Blue is a valuable color and is always at a premium in the garden. The showy 3" to 4" flat flowerheads of Stokes' aster have two concentric rows of ragged blue rays and fuzzy white centers. The attractive buds resemble straw flowers.

Plant in average to rich, moist soil in full sun or light shade. Stokes' asters are easy to grow, long-lived perennials that form dense, multi-crowned clumps. Divide for propagation or when plants get overcrowded.
NATIVE HABITAT AND RANGE: Low, wet pine woods, bottomlands, and ditches from North Carolina to Florida and Louisiana.
USDA HARDINESS ZONES: 5 to 9

HABIT, USE, AND COMPANIONS:
Stokes' asters produce broad rosettes of shiny, green, lance-shaped leaves, each of which has a conspicuous white midvein. Each 1′ to 2′ branched stalk bears several flowers in summer. Plants grow from cord-like white roots. Stokes' asters create a dramatic show for several months in summer. Combine them with small flowers and fine-textured foliage such as verbenas, penstemons, yarrows, and ornamental grasses. In light shade plant them with phlox, columbines (*Aquilegia* species), ferns, and hostas.

CULTIVARS AND RELATED SPECIES: 'Blue Danube' has 5″ lavender-blue flowers, 'Blue Star' has deep sky-blue flowers. 'Silver Moon' has creamy white flowers. 'Wyoming' has rich blue-violet flowers.

Stokes' aster

Plant in average to rich, moist but well-drained, acidic soil in full sun or light shade. In limy soils plants become anemic and yellow.

NATIVE HABITAT AND RANGE:
Open woods, meadows, clearings, and roadsides from North Carolina to Georgia.

USDA HARDINESS ZONES: 3 to 9

HABIT, USE, AND COMPANIONS:
Carolina bush peas have 3′ to 5′ stalks and showy, yellow, pea-like flowers. Plants form multi-stemmed clumps from woody, fibrous-rooted crowns. Place them in the middle or rear of borders with meadow rues (*Thalictrum* species), catmints (*Nepeta* species), hardy cranesbills, phlox, and peonies. At the edge of a

Thermopsis villosa (also known as *T. caroliniana*)
CAROLINA BUSH PEA
A Carolina bush pea in full bloom is an exceptional sight. Its narrow, upright stems and alternate gray-green leaves, fuzzy underneath, are crowned by tightly packed spikes of bright lemon-yellow flowers. Each leaf has 3 oval leaflets joined to a short stalk. The seed heads are showy in winter, and chickadees and sparrows relish the seeds.

SUN

SUN

The tall, lemon-yellow spires of Carolina bush pea are dazzling in summer.

meadow or woodland, plant them with wild sennas, bluestar, bowman's-root, bergamot, and grasses.
CULTIVARS AND RELATED SPECIES: Mountain false lupine (*T. rhombifolia*) grows to 2′ тo 3′ tall with 6″- to 8″-long, vivid yellow flowers. It is found in wet meadows and well-drained sites from Washington to Montana, south to Colorado and Nevada. Zones 4 to 8.

Tradescantia subaspera
SPIDERWORT

Spiderworts are named for the web-like hairs in the centers of the flowers. They produce hundreds of attractive, satiny, 3-petaled flowers in clusters atop succulent, jointed stems. Flower color varies from purple, lavender, and blue to pink, rose-red, and white. Each flower lasts only half a day, closing by early afternoon.

Plant in average to rich, moist but well-drained soil in full to light shade. Plants grow well in partial shade but do not flower as long. After flowering the clumps flop, so cut them to the ground. They produce new foliage in late summer or autumn. Plants increase quickly to form dense clumps and self-sow readily.
NATIVE HABITAT AND RANGE: Rich woods, clearings, and roadsides from Virginia and Illinois, south to Florida and Alabama.

USDA HARDINESS ZONES: 4 to 9
HABIT, USE, AND COMPANIONS: Spiderwort (*T. subaspera*) is the largest and stoutest of the spiderworts. Plants grow to $3\frac{1}{2}′$ from thick, upright stems with broad, gray-green leaves and 1″ blue to purple flowers. Plant spiderworts in formal gardens with hardy cranesbills, bergenias, phlox, and ornamental grasses. In meadows or woodland edges, plant them in drifts or scattered clumps with persistent plants like wild bleeding heart, mountain mints, bluestars, goldenrods, and ferns.
CULTIVARS AND RELATED SPECIES: Virginia spiderwort (*T. virginiana*) is a delicate plant with slender 2′ to 3′ stems and 12″ deep green leaves. The flowers are blue to purple. Found in moist, open woods, flood plains, meadows, and prairies from Maine and Wisconsin, south to Georgia and Missouri. Zones 4 to 9.

Vernonia altissima
TALL IRONWEED

The broad, violet flower clusters of ironweed demand attention in the summer and autumn garden. Most species have numerous tall, stiff stems clothed in deep green, lance-shaped leaves. The name ironweed presumably arises from the prominent rust-red hairs in the spent flower heads and on the

SUN

SUN

Tall ironweed

USDA HARDINESS ZONES: 4 to 8
HABIT, USE, AND COMPANIONS:
Tall ironweed is the giant of the group, with 4′ to 10′ stems and dense, broad, flattened clusters of soft-violet flowers in late summer and autumn. Plant in rich, moist soil in full sun. Ironweeds are commanding border plants. Plant them with yarrows (*Achillea* species), cannas, lilies, salvias, and iris. They are equally well suited to meadow and prairie gardens or along the banks of ponds. Combine them with hibiscus, phlox, blue lobelia (*Lobelia siphilitica*), Joe-pye weeds, turtleheads, asters, goldenrods, and grasses.

CULTIVARS AND RELATED SPECIES:
Narrow-leaf ironweed (*V. angustifolia*) has 1″, deep violet heads carried in broad, open clusters on wide, shrub-like clumps from 2′ to 4′ tall. The 6″ to 8″ leaves are narrowly lance-shaped and droop slightly on the stem. Found in sandy meadows, open woods, savannas, and roadsides from North Carolina to Florida and Mississippi. Zones 4 to 9.

fruits. Plants are grown from woody, fibrous-rooted crowns.

Plant in rich, evenly moist soil in full sun or light shade. Plants are easy to grow and thrive in most garden situations. The clumps get tall and wide, but seldom need staking or division. Tall ironweed is sometimes listed as *V. gigantea*.

NATIVE HABITAT AND RANGE:
Found in wet meadows and prairies, wetland edges, pond margins, and ditches from New York, Michigan, and Nebraska, south to Georgia and Louisiana.

Veronicastrum virginicum
CULVER'S ROOT
The erect, creamy white candelabra spikes on 3′ to 6′ stems make a dramatic show. The toothed, lance-shaped leaves are borne in tiered whorls on the

stout stems. Culver's root is often placed in the genus *Veronica*, to which it is closely related.

Plant in rich, moist soil in full sun or light shade. Established plants tolerate short periods of drought. Plants form dense, multi-stemmed clumps that are easily divided in early spring or autumn. The dried seed heads ornament the winter landscape.

NATIVE HABITAT AND RANGE: Open woods, low meadows, prairies, floodplains, and outcroppings from Ontario and Manitoba, south to Georgia and Louisiana.

USDA HARDINESS ZONES: 3 to 9

HABIT, USE, AND COMPANIONS: The upright spikes of Culver's root add lift and excitement to the middle or rear of beds and borders. Plants grow from woody crowns with thick, fleshy roots. In borders and formal situations combine them with turtleheads, hibiscus, coneflowers, and yarrows. Try milkweeds, bee balms, ironweeds, anise hyssop (*Agastache foeniculum*), rattlesnake master (*Eryngium yuccifolium*), asters, goldenrods, and grasses in meadow and prairie gardens.

CULTIVARS AND RELATED SPECIES: The *rosea* variety, sometimes listed as 'Roseum' cultivar, has pale rose-pink flowers. Soft blue selections are seen but are likely to be from the European species.

Culver's root

Yucca filamentosa
THREAD-LEAF YUCCA, ADAM'S NEEDLE

Yuccas are quintessential desert plants, but they grow throughout North America. They have tall, oval flower clusters and rosettes of sword-shaped, blue-green leaves. The nodding, creamy-white, waxen bells have 3 petals and 3 petal-like sepals.

Plant yuccas in average to rich, well-drained soil in full sun or light shade. They are long-lived, drought-tolerant, and carefree. After flowering, the main crown dies but auxiliary shoots are pro-

SUN

SUN

Thread-leaf yucca is a quintessential desert plant—long-lived and carefree.

duced from the rhizome and perpetuate the clump.

NATIVE HABITAT AND RANGE: Sand dunes, outcroppings, and pine barrens in the coastal plain and mountains from Maryland to Georgia.

USDA HARDINESS ZONES: 4 to 10

HABIT, USE, AND COMPANIONS: The erect, multi-branched bloom stalks rise 5' to 15' above the stiff, 2' to 2½' needle-like leaves. The nodding, creamy white flowers are waxy in texture and are 2" long. They grow from a woody crown with fleshy roots. Plant yuccas in dry soil or rock gardens, as accent plantings, or in seaside gardens. Contrast the stiff foliage with soft or delicate plants such as verbenas, winecups, prickly pear cactus (*Opuntia humifusa*), sages, gaura, gaillardia, and evening primrose (*Oenothera* species).

CULTIVARS AND RELATED SPECIES: 'Bright Edge' has yellow-variegated leaves. Soapweed (*Y. glauca*) has narrow, 2', stiff, gray-green leaves crowned by dense clusters of nodding, creamy white to pale pink flowers on 2' to 3' stems. Plant in average to rich, well-drained soil in full sun or light shade. Found on dry prairies and plains from North Dakota and Wyoming, south to Missouri, Texas, and Arizona. Zones 3 to 9.

Aiken, George D. *Pioneering With Wildflowers*. Prentice-Hall, Englewood Cliffs, New Jersey, 1968, 1996.

Armitage, Allan. *Herbaceous Perennial Plants: A Treatise on Their Identification, Culture, and Garden Attributes*. Varsity Press, Athens, Georgia, 1989.

Art, Henry W. *A Garden of Wildflowers: 101 Native Species and How to Grow Them*. Storey Communications, Pownal, Vermont, 1986.

Art, Henry W. *The Wildflower Gardener's Guide* (4 regional editions: Northeast and Mid-Atlantic; California and desert Southwest;.Midwest and Great Plains; and Pacific Northwest and Rockie Mountains). Garden Way Publishing, Pownal, Vermont, 1987, 1990, 1991.

Barr, Claude A. *Jewels of the Plains: Wildflowers of the Great Plains Grasslands and Hills*. University of Minnesota Press, Minneapolis, 1983.

Beaubaire, Nancy, editor. *Native Perennials: North American Beauties*. Brooklyn Botanic Garden, Brooklyn, New York, 1996.

Bruce, Hal. *How to Grow Wildflowers and Wild Shrubs and Trees in Your Own Garden*. Knopf, New York, 1976.

Burrell, C. Colston, editor. *Ferns: Wild Things Make a Comeback in the Garden*. Brooklyn Botanic Garden, Brooklyn, New York, 1994, 1995.

Burrell, C. Colston. *A Gardener's Encyclopedia of Wildflowers: An Organic Guide to Choosing and Growing Over 150 Beautiful Wildflowers*. Rodale Press, Emmaus, Pennsylvania, 1997.

Burrell, C. Colston, editor. *The Natural Water Garden: Pools Ponds, Marshes & Bogs for Backyards Everywhere*. Brooklyn Botanic Garden, Brooklyn, New York, 1997.

Burrell, C. Colston, editor. *Woodland Gardens: Shade Gets Chic*. Brooklyn Botanic Garden, Brooklyn, New York, 1995.

Diekelmann, John and Robert Schuster. *Natural Landscaping: Designing With Native Plant Communities*. McGraw-Hill, New York, 1982.

Dormon, Caroline. *Natives Preferred: Native Trees and Flowers for Every Location.* Claitor's Book Store, Baton Rouge, Louisiana, 1965.

Druse, Kenneth with Margaret Roach. *The Natural Habitat Garden.* Clarkson Potter, New York, 1994.

Ferreniea, Viki, *Wildflowers in Your Garden.* Random House, New York, 1993.

Jensen, Jens. *Siftings.* Johns Hopkins University Press, Baltimore. 1939, 1990.

Kress, Stephen W., editor. *Bird Gardens: Welcoming Wild Birds to Your Yard.* Brooklyn Botanic Garden, Brooklyn, New York, 1998.

Lovejoy, Ann. *Naturalistic Gardening: Reflecting the Planting Patterns of Nature.* Sasquatch Books, Seattle, 1998.

Marinelli, Janet, editor. *The Environmental Gardener.* Brooklyn Botanic Garden, Brooklyn, New York, 1992.

Marinelli, Janet, editor. *Going Native: Biodiversity in Our Own Backyards.* Brooklyn Botanic Garden, Brooklyn, New York, 1994, 1996.

Roach, Margaret, editor. *The Natural Lawn & Alternatives.* Brooklyn Botanic Garden, Brooklyn, New York, 1993.

Mickel, John. *Ferns for American Gardens.* MacMillan, New York, 1994.

Miles, Bebe. *Wildflower Perennials for Your Garden: A Detailed Guide to Years of Bloom From America's Long-neglected Native Heritage.* Hawthorne Books, New York, 1976.

Phillips, Roger and Martyn Rix. *Perennials* (2 volumes). Random House, New York, 1991.

Smith, J. Robert with Beatrice S. Smith, *The Prairie Garden: 70 Native Plants You Can Grow in Town or Country.* University of Wisconsin Press, Madison, 1980.

Wasowski, Sally with Andy Wasowski. *Gardening with Native Plants of the South.* Taylor Publishing Company, Dallas, 1994.

COLLECTORS NURSERY
16804 N.E. 102nd
Avenue
Battleground, WA
98604
(360) 574-3832

FORESTFARM
990 Tetherow Road
Williams, OR 97544
(541) 846-7269
www.forestfarm.com

HENRY'S PLANT FARM
4522 132nd Street S.E.
Snohomish, WA 98296
(425) 337-8120
www.henrysplantfarm.-
com

LANDSCAPE ALTERNATIVES, INC.
1705 St. Albans Street
Roseville, MN 55113
(612) 488-3142

MISSOURI WILDFLOWERS NURSERY
9814 Pleasant Hill Road
Jefferson City, MO
65109
(573) 496-3492

NATIVE GARDENS
5737 Fisher Lane
Greenback, TN 37742
(423) 856-0220

THE NATURAL GARDEN
38W443 Highway 64
St. Charles, IL 60175
(630) 584-0150

NICHE GARDENS
1111 Dawson Road
Chapel Hill, NC 27516
(919) 967-0078
www.nichegdn.com

PLANTS OF THE SOUTHWEST
Agua Fria Road
Route 6, Box 11A
Santa Fe, MN 87501
(800) 788-7333
www.plantsofthesouth-
west.com

PRAIRIE MOON NURSERY
Rt. 3, Box 163
Winona, MN 55987
(507) 452-1362

PRAIRIE NURSERY
P.O. Box 306
Westfield, WI 53964
(800) 476-9453
www.prairienursery.com

PRAIRIE RESTORATIONS, INC.
P.O. Box 327
Princeton, MN 55371
(612) 389-4342

SUNLIGHT GARDENS
174 Golden Lane
Andersonville, TN
37705
(423) 494-8237

TRANSPLANT NURSERY
1586 Parkertown Rd.
Lavonia, GA 30553
(706) 356-8947

WE-DU NURSERIES
Route 5, Box 724
Marion, NC 28752
(828) 738-8300
www.we-du.com

WOODLANDERS, INC.
1128 Colleton Ave.
Aiken, SC 29801
(803) 648-7522

HENRY W. ART is a garden writer, Samuel Fessenden Clarke Professor of Biology, and the director of the Center for Environmental Studies at Williams College in Williamstown, Massachusetts. He is the author of *A Garden of Wildflowers* (Storey Communications, 1986) and four different regional editions of *Wildflower Gardener's Guide* (Garden Way Publishing, 1987, 1990, 1991). He has a doctorate in forestry from Yale University.

C. COLSTON BURRELL is a designer, writer, photographer and naturalist. A lifelong gardener and advocate for native plants, he has written and taught about design and plants for over 20 years. He has edited several Brooklyn Botanic Garden handbooks, including *Ferns: Wild Things Make a Comeback in the Garden* (1994, 1995), *The Natural Water Garden: Pools Ponds, Marshes &*

Bogs for Backyards Everywhere (1997), *Woodland Gardens: Shade Gets Chic* (1995), and *The Shady Border: Knockout Plants That Light up the Shadows* (1998). He is the author of *Perennial Combinations: Stunning Combinations That Make Your Garden Look Fantastic Right From the Start* (Rodale Press, 1999) and the award-winning *A Gardener's Encyclopedia of Wildflowers: An Organic Guide to Choosing and Growing Over 150 Beautiful Wildflowers* (Rodale Press, 1997). He has graduate degrees in horticulture and landscape architecture. Cole recently moved his garden from Minneapolis to the Blue Ridge Mountains near Charlottesville, Virginia.

KIM HAWKS is a wildflower gardener who started her own nursery, Niche Gardens, when she discovered that the

only wildflowers available were either poor quality or had been dug from the wild. Niche Gardens in Chapel Hill, North Carolina, is a leading mail order nursery, growing North American natives with an emphasis on southeastern perennials. Kim is also a garden designer and writer, whose articles have appeared in *Fine Gardening*, *The Herb Companion*, and *North Carolina Wildlife*.

JOAN FEELY is the curator of the Fern Valley Native Plant Collection at the United States National Arboretum, where she has worked since 1986. Before moving to Washington, D.C., she lived and gardened in New York, Maine, Massachusetts, and Alaska.

MADELEINE KEEVE, now living and gardening in Portland, Oregon, was formerly a gardener at Wave Hill in the Bronx, New York. She has also contributed to *Horticulture* magazine, *Gardener's World of Bulbs* (Brooklyn Botanic Garden, 1991), and *Low-Maintenance Gardening* (Sunset Books, 1998).

CAROLE OTTESEN is a garden writer and designer whose work has appeared in many magazines, including *House Beautiful*, *Horticulture*, *Garden Design*, and *Fine Gardening*. Her latest book is *Growing and Cooking With Plants That Heal* (Ballantine Books, 1999). She is also the author of *The Native Plant Primer* (Harmony, 1995), *Ornamental Grasses: The Amber Wave* (McGraw-Hill, 1989, 1995), and *Gardening With Style*, with coauthors Graham Rose and Peter King (Bloomsbury Press, 1988). Her two-acre organic garden in Potomac, Maryland, includes ornamental

grasses, several perennial borders, a medicinal plants garden, an herb and vegetable garden, a natural woodland garden, a moss lawn, and a vast array of plants, including many native to eastern North America.

JAMES STEVENSON is working and studying at the Royal Botanic Gardens, Kew, in London. For two years he worked as curator and garden manager of Juniper Level Botanic Garden near Raleigh, North Carolina. He also built and managed a small specialty nursery and garden center and designed and maintained the perennial displays at Fearington Gardens in Pittsboro, North Carolina. In addition, James worked as an intern at the North Carolina Botanical Garden in Chapel Hill after earning a degree in plant ecology from the University of the South in Sewanee, Tennessee.

PHOTO CREDITS

C. COLSTON BURRELL: pages 8 (right), 20, 42, 43, 54, 58, 59, 89, 93, and 98

DAVID CAVAGNARO: pages 5, 10, 13, 21, 24, 27, 31, 33, 35, 37, 39, 44, 47, 61, 65, 67, 68, 69, 71, 82, 83, 85, 95, 96, and 99

ALAN & LINDA DETRICK: pages 29, 38 (left), 49, 50, 51, 60, 63, 64, 74, 79, 81, and 91

CHRISTINE M. DOUGLAS: pages 9 (right) and 15

SUSAN M. GLASCOCK: pages 7, 9 (left), 48, 70, 77, 87, and 92

PAMELA HARPER: pages 45, 56, 62, and 100

CAROLE OTTESEN: pages 28 and 53

JERRY PAVIA: cover, pages 1, 8 (left), 14, 23, 34, 38 (right), 57, 66, 72, and 73

VIRGINIA R. WEILER: page 19

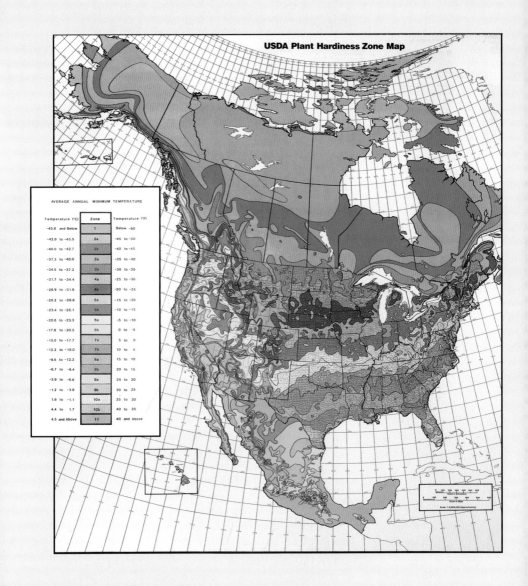

USDA Plant Hardiness Zone Map

AVERAGE ANNUAL MINIMUM TEMPERATURE

Temperature (°C)	Zone	Temperature (°F)
-45.6 and Below	1	Below -50
-42.8 to -45.5	2a	-45 to -50
-40.0 to -42.7	2b	-40 to -45
-37.3 to -40.0	3a	-35 to -40
-34.5 to -37.2	3b	-30 to -35
-31.7 to -34.4	4a	-25 to -30
-28.9 to -31.6	4b	-20 to -25
-26.2 to -28.8	5a	-15 to -20
-23.4 to -26.1	5b	-10 to -15
-20.6 to -23.3	6a	-5 to -10
-17.8 to -20.5	6b	0 to -5
-15.0 to -17.7	7a	5 to 0
-12.3 to -15.0	7b	10 to 5
-9.5 to -12.2	8a	15 to 10
-6.7 to -9.4	8b	20 to 15
-3.9 to -6.6	9a	25 to 20
-1.2 to -3.8	9b	30 to 25
1.6 to -1.1	10a	35 to 30
4.4 to 1.7	10b	40 to 35
4.5 and Above	11	40 and Above

BROOKLYN BOTANIC GARDEN

MORE

BOOKS ON

WILDFLOWER

GARDENS

BROOKLYN BOTANIC GARDEN

handbooks are available at a discount

from our web site

www.bbg.org/gardenemporium/

OR CALL
(718) 623-7200

Watch our garden grow

in your very own mailbox!

From Great Neck to Great Bend, Big River to Little Creek, over 20,000 people in all 50 states enjoy the bountiful benefits of membership in the **Brooklyn Botanic Garden** – including our renowned gardening publications.

Brooklyn Botanic Garden Membership

The splendor that makes the Brooklyn Botanic Garden one of the finest in the world can be a regular part of your life. BBG membership brings you subscriptions to some of the liveliest, best-researched, and most practical gardening publications anywhere – including the next entries in our acclaimed 21st-Century Gardening Series (currently published quarterly). BBG publications are written by expert gardeners and horticulturists, and have won prestigious *Quill and Trowel* awards for excellence in garden publishing.

Plants & Gardens News – practical and suggestions from BBG experts.

SUBSCRIBER $35

(Library and Institution Rate $60)

* A full year of *21st-Century Gardening Series* handbooks
* A year's subscription to *Plants & Gardens News*
* Reciprocal privileges at botanical gardens across the country

FAMILY/DUAL $50

All benefits of SUBSCRIBER, plus

* Membership card for free admission for two adult members and their children under 16
* 10% discount at the Terrace Cafe & Garden Gift Shop
* Free parking for four visits
* Discounts on classes, trips and tours

SIGNATURE $125

All benefits of FAMILY, plus

* Your choice of a Signature Plant from our annual catalog of rare and unique shrubs, perennials and house plants
* 12 free parking passes
* A special BBG gift calendar

BBG Catalog – quarterly listing of classes, workshops and tours in the and abroad, all at a discount.

SPONSOR $300

All benefits of SIGNATURE, plus

* Your choice of <u>two</u> Signature Plants
* Four complimentary one-time guest passes
* 24 free parking passes
* Invitations to special receptions

GARDENING BOOKS FOR THE NEXT CENTURY

Brooklyn Botanic Garden's 21st-Century Gardening Series explore frontiers of ecological gardening - offering practical, step-by-step tips on creating environmentally sensitive and beautiful gardens for the 1990s and the new century.

Spring 1999
Please send in this form or contact BBG
for current membership information, higher levels and benefits.

21st-Century Gardening Series – the n handbooks in this acclaimed library.